名作映画を英語で読む
ローマの休日
(字幕対訳付)

藤田英時 編著

宝島社

目　次

■序章「ローマの休日」で楽しく英話力アップ……5
本書での表記のしかた……10

■第1部「ローマの休日」シーン別リーディング……11

Scene 1	ニュース映画	「アン王女のヨーロッパ親善旅行」……12
Scene 2	大使館・接見室	「アン王女の公式歓迎会・舞踏会」…16
Scene 3	大使館・アン王女の寝室	「アン王女のヒステリー」……20
Scene 4	大使館・アン王女の寝室	「医師の注射」……28
Scene 5	ホテルの一室	「記者仲間のポーカー」……32
Scene 6	フォロ・ロマーノ	「ジョーとアン王女の初めての出会い」…36
Scene 7	タクシー	「タクシーの行き先」……40
Scene 8	マルグッタ通り・ジョーのアパートの前	「運転手とのやり取り」……44
Scene 9	ジョーのアパート・室内	「ジョーとアン王女とパジャマ」……48
Scene 10	大使館・大使の書斎	「アン王女の失踪」……54
Scene 11	ジョーのアパート・室内	「ジョーの寝過ごし」……56
Scene 12	アメリカン・ニュース社のオフィス	「ジョーの遅刻」……58
Scene 13	ヘネシーのオフィス	「ジョーの言い訳と支局長の追及」……60
Scene 14	ヘネシーのオフィス	「ジョーと支局長の賭け」……70
Scene 15	ジョーのアパート・中庭	「ジョーの借金話」……76
Scene 16	ジョーのアパート・室内	「ジョーとアン王女の自己紹介」……80
Scene 17	彫刻家のスタジオ	「相棒のカメラマンへの電話」……88

Scene18	ジョーのアパート・室内	「掃除婦のアン王女への説教」	………92
Scene19	ジョーのアパート・テラス	「ジョーとアン王女のお別れ」	………94
Scene20	ジョーのアパート・室内	「さようなら」	………98
Scene21	ジョーのアパート・中庭	「アン王女の借金」	………100
Scene22	横町・市場	「アン王女の青空市場めぐり」	………104
Scene23	理髪店	「アン王女の大胆ショートカット」	……106
Scene24	バー・電話	「電話使用中」	………110
Scene25	トレビの泉	「ジョーのカメラ探し」	………112
Scene26	理髪店	「カット終了とダンスへの誘い」	………114
Scene27	スペイン広場	「アン王女とアイスクリームと花」	………118
Scene28	スペイン広場の階段	「アン王女の告白と休日の始まり」	…122
Scene29	ロッカズ・カフェ	「お互いの詮索と相棒カメラマン」	128
Scene30	ロッカズ・カフェの中	「ジョーとアービングの密約」	………138
Scene31	ロッカズ・カフェのテーブル	「アン王女の初めてのタバコ」	……142
Scene32	ヴェネツィア広場の通り	「スクーターの乱暴運転」	………148
Scene33	警察署	「ジョーたちの必死の説得」	………150
Scene34	サンタマリア イン コスメディン教会・真実の口	「真実の口の言い伝え」	………154
Scene35	モルガーニ通り・祈りの壁	「かなわぬ願い事」	………158
Scene36	サンタンジェロ城下の船	「パーティでの大騒動」	………164
Scene37	テヴェレ川・橋の下のアーチ	「ジョーとアン王女の初めてのキス」	…170
Scene38	ジョーのアパート・室内	「ジョーとアン王女の心中」	………172

Scene39	アービングの車の中	「ジョーとアン王女の切ない別れ」	……178
Scene40	大使館・アン王女の寝室	「威厳のあるアン王女」	……180
Scene41	ジョーのアパート・室内	「支局長のジョーへの追及」	……184
Scene42	ジョーのアパート・室内	「アン王女の写真」	……192
Scene43	大使館・応接室	「アン王女の記者会見」	……198

「ローマの休日」の名所ガイド……206

■第2部「ローマの休日」のリスニング
　　　　　　　発音の変化7つの公式……207

序章

「ローマの休日」で楽しく英話力アップ

■本書は完全英文シナリオ＋初の字幕対訳

　実生活に必要な生きた本物の英語、それを楽しみながら学ぶことができるのが名作映画です。その中でも「ローマの休日」は最高の素材と言えるでしょう。

　本書は「ローマの休日」の完全英文シナリオに字幕対訳が付けられています。初の字幕対訳本です。

■本書の内容と特長

●実際に話されているセリフを掲載

　シナリオ本やインターネット上のシナリオ、ＤＶＤの英語字幕などは、実際のセリフとはかなり違っています。

　しかし、本書では実際に話されたままの英語を掲載しています。表現の確認やリスニングのチェックなどに役立ちます。

●シーンを細かく分けて写真を数多く掲載

　英文ばかり埋まっていると読みづらいものですが、本書ではシーンを細かく分けて、そのシーンの写真とセリフを掲載しています。ストーリーのポイントや展開がよく分かり、英文が理解しやすくなります。

●実際に表示される字幕を掲載

　従来のシナリオ本は英文1行単位の対訳付きですが、本書は「字幕対訳付き」です。画面に実際に表示される字幕に相当し、英語の意味がつかみやすい要約になっています。学習に最適なように、原文に忠実ながらもこなれた日本語にしています（→9ページ）。

　一般に映画の字幕は、いき過ぎた意訳や誤訳などが多く、学習には適していませんが、本書の字幕対訳ではそのようなことはありません。

　また、ふつう字幕には表示されない短い表現や外国語（ここではイタリア語）もカッコ付きで訳しています。

●解説付きで簡単に読み進められる

　映画のセリフを分析してみると8割くらいは中学英語です。中学で学ぶ必修語彙と基本語彙で約1500語の範囲で、使われている単語は知っているものが大半です。「ローマの休日」では9割以上です。

　やさしい英語に加え、表現やニュアンスなどの解説を詳しく付けていますので、簡単に読み進められます。

■本書の活用法

本書をいろいろと活用すれば、楽しく英語力アップが図れます。

●本書だけを使う場合
・映画のシーンを思い浮かべながら気楽に読み進む。
・字幕対訳で大筋をつかんでから英語表現や細かいニュアンスなどを理解する。

「ローマの休日」では、掛け言葉がたくさんでてきますが、そのニュアンスを英語のままで味わいたいものです。

swallow	「呑み込む」と「理解する」
spill	「こぼす」と「秘密をもらす」
slip	「すべる」と「口をすべらす」
hurt	「傷つく」と「困る」
grand	「素敵な」と「1000ドル」
development	「開発」と「写真の現像」
shave	「ヒゲをそる」と「危機一髪」

・名セリフや好きなセリフを覚える。
　It's just what I wanted.

・会話で使える表現を覚える。
　次の名セリフを覚えておけば、場所だけを変えれば、

海外旅行やどこかに招かれたときに使えます。
　　Rome! By all means, Rome!
　　I will cherish my visit here,
　　in memory, as long as I live.

●ビデオやＤＶＤと併用する場合
・好きなシーンを聞き取って、実際のセリフと比較してリスニング力アップを図る。
・好きなシーンのセリフに合わせてスピーキングの練習をする。

●字幕に興味がある場合
・字幕がいかに省略されているかが分かる。字幕だけで映画を観るのとセリフが聞き取れて分かって観るのとでは格段の相違があります。
・ビデオやDVDの字幕と本書の字幕とどう違うか比べてみると面白い。翻訳者によって、かなり違うことが分かります。
・好きなセリフを自分で字幕に訳してみると面白い。セリフの英語をよく理解し、意味を的確につかんでいないと「いい字幕」はできません。英語と日本語の実力が同時につきます。

■本書での表記のしかた

●主なキャラクターの略称

ANN ： アン（某国の王女）
JOE ： ジョー（新聞記者）
IRV ： アービン（Irving：写真家）
HEN ： 支局長（Hennessy：ジョーの上司）
GIO ： ジョバンニ（Giovanni：ジョーの大家）
CTS ： 伯爵夫人（Countess）
DOC ： 医者（Doctor）
M.C. ： 式部官（Master of Ceremonies）
AMB ： 駐伊大使（Ambassador to Italy）
ADM ： 海軍大将（Admiral）
GEN ： 将軍（General）
SEC ： 秘書（Secretary）
OFF ： 大使館職員（Officer）
DRV ： タクシー運転手（Taxi Driver）

●字幕対訳

・映画の字幕と同じ形式でセリフの要約。
・カッコ内は字幕としては表示されないセリフ。
・写真横の英文セリフは発音のまま（発音表記）。
・その訳は英文に近い訳で字幕対訳とは別。
・その字幕対訳のほうは簡略化された訳。

第1部

「ローマの休日」
シーン別リーディング

Scene 1

ニュース映画
「アン王女のヨーロッパ親善旅行」

She gets a royal welcome from the British...

「イギリス市民から
　熱烈な歓迎を受け…」

COMMENTATOR :
Paramount News brings you a special coverage of Princess Ann's visit to London.
The first stop on her much publicized goodwill tour of European capitals.
She gets a royal welcome from the British, as thousands cheer the gracious young member of one of Europe's oldest ruling families.
After three days of continuous activity and a visit to Buckingham Palace, Ann flew to Amsterdam, where Her Royal Highness dedicated the new International Aid Building and christened an ocean liner.
Then went to Paris, where she attended many official functions designed to cement trade relations between her country and the Western European nations.

And so to Rome, the Eternal City...
「そして永遠の都ローマへ…」

解説者 :
  "ニュース速報"
  アン王女ロンドン訪問へ
  ここは親善旅行
  最初の訪問地であり
  イギリス市民は熱烈に歓迎
  由緒ある王家の一員に
  声援を送ります
  3日間の精力的な活動の後
  アムステルダムへ
  そこで外航船の
  進水式に出席

  次のパリでは
  数々の公式行事に参加
  ヨーロッパ各国との
  貿易関係を強固なものに

COMMENTATOR :
>And so to Rome, the Eternal City, where the Princess' visit was marked by a spectacular military parade, highlighted by the band of the crack Bersaglieri Regiment.
>The smiling young Princess showed no sign of the strain of the week's continuous public appearances.
>And at her country's Embassy that evening, a formal reception and ball, in her honor, was given by her country's Ambassador to Italy.

このトリビアで通になろう!
● 当時、映画上映の前に必ずニュースを流していた。アン王女の親善旅行の映像は観客が映画の本編ではなくニュース映画と思わせるためのお遊び的な演出。

このニュアンスを味わう!
● アン王女のことを Princess Ann, Ann, She, Her Royal Highness, the Princess, the smiling young Princess と使いわけている。英語では同じ単語の繰り返しをさけ、同じ意味で別の単語を用いるのがよいとされる。

解説者：

  そして永遠の都ローマへ
  王女の来訪を祝うパレードに
  音楽隊の演奏が花を添えます

  多忙な日程にも
  疲れは見えません

  その夜 王女を歓迎する
  舞踏会が駐伊大使によって
  開かれました

このセリフ、会話にいただき！
● ball は「正式な舞踏会」のことで、私的なものは dance を使う。「宴会場」は ballroom で「社交ダンス」は ballroom dancing。ball には「楽しいひと時」という意味もあり、Have a ball. で「楽しんで」。We had a ball at the event.（行事で楽しい時を過ごした）。

Scene 2 大使館・接見室
「アン王女の公式歓迎会・舞踏会」

Her Royal Highness.
「王女様」

M.C. : Sua Altezza Reale — Her Royal Highness.

His Excellency, the Papal Nuncio. Monsignor Altomonte.
ANN : Eccellenza, piacere di conoscerLa.
ALT : Grazie della bonta di vostra Altezza Reale...grazie.
M.C. : Sir Hugo Macey de Farmington.
ANN : Good evening, Sir Hugo.
HUG : Good evening, Your Royal Highness.
M.C. : His Highness, the Maharajah of Khanipur, and Rajkumari.
ANN : I'm so glad that you could come.
RAJ : Thank you.
MAH : Thank you, Madam.
M.C. : Freiherr Erika Messingfroner, Berngton.
ANN : Guten Abend.
M.C. : Prince Istvar Barlossy Nagyvaros.
ANN : How do you do?

I'm so glad that you could come.
「おいでいただきとても嬉しく思います」

式部官　：王女様のお出ましです

　　　　　アルトモンテ教皇大使閣下

アン　　：はじめまして
閣下　　：お招き感謝します

式部官　：ヒューゴ・ファーミントン卿
アン　　：こんばんは
ヒュー卿：こんばんは
式部官　：カニプールのマハラジャご夫妻

アン　　：歓迎します
マハ妃　：感謝します
マハ王　：感謝します
式部官　：フリヘル・エリカ卿
アン　　：こんばんは
式部官　：イスバー・バロシー王子
アン　　：はじめまして

M.C. :	Ihre Hoheit der Furst und die Furstin von und zu Lichtenstichenholz.
ANN :	Guten Abend. Freut mich sehr.
M.C. :	Sir Hari Singh and Khara Singh...
ANN :	...So happy...
M.C. :	The Count and Countess von Marstrand.
ANN :	Good evening, Countess. Good evening.
M.C. :	Senore and Senora Joaquin de Camoes.
ANN :	Good evening.
M.C. :	Hassan El Din Pasha.
ANN :	How do you do?
AMB :	Your Highness.
ADM :	E per carita voglio assolutamente morire sulla nave, si...perche...perche...

このセリフ、会話にいただき！
● I'm so glad that you could come.（おいでいただきとても嬉しく思います）は、非常にていねいな言い方。カジュアルなら、Thank you for coming. または Thanks for coming.
このイタリア語がわかればもっと楽しめる！
● Piacere は「嬉しい」の意味で、初対面のときに使われる。Piacere di conoscerLa. は Pleased to meet you. と同じ。Grazie は英語の Thank you。

式部官　：イレ・ホハイト・デル・ファルトご夫妻

(アン　　：こんばんは　光栄です)
式部官　：ハリ・シン卿ご夫妻
アン　　：…光栄です…
式部官　：マーストランド伯爵ご夫妻
アン　　：こんばんは　こんばんは
式部官　：カモーシュのホアモンご夫妻
アン　　：こんばんは
式部官　：エル・ディン長官
アン　　：はじめまして

大使　　：王女様

(大将　　：私は船の上で死にとうございます)

このニュアンスを味わう!
- **So happy** は「たいへん嬉しく思います」「光栄です」といった意味。王室の人たちなどが使う。

このトリビアで通になろう!
- 舞踏会のシーンでは本物のイタリアの貴族が出演した。その出演料はチャリティに寄付された。
- ダンスシーンでアン王女と踊っている海軍大将は「絶対、船の上で死にたい」と話している。

Scene 3　大使館・アン王女の寝室
「アン王女のヒステリー」

But I'm not two hundred years old.
「でも私は年寄りではないのよ」

ANN : I hate this nightgown.
　　　I hate all my nightgowns, and I hate all my underwear, too.
CTS : My dear, you have lovely things.
ANN : But I'm not two hundred years old.
　　　Why can't I sleep in pajamas?
CTS : Pajamas!
ANN : Just the top part.
　　　Did you know there are people who sleep with absolutely nothing on at all?
CTS : I rejoice to say that I did not.
ANN : Listen!
CTS : Oh, and your slippers!
　　　Please put on your slippers and come away from the window.
　　　Your milk and crackers.
ANN : Everything we do is so wholesome.
CTS : They'll help you to sleep.
ANN : I'm too tired to sleep — can't sleep a wink.

I'm too tired to sleep. I shan't sleep a wink.

「疲れすぎて
　眠れそうにないわ」

アン　　：イヤなネグリジェ
　　　　　　私のネグリジェはどれも大嫌い
　　　　　　下着も
夫人　　：ご立派なものばかりです
アン　　：私は年寄りではないのよ
　　　　　　パジャマで寝たいわ
夫人　　：パジャマだなんて
アン　　：それも上だけを
　　　　　　何も着ないで寝る人がいるって
　　　　　　知ってた？
夫人　　：存じ上げません
アン　　：聞こえる？
夫人　　：まあ　スリッパを
　　　　　　これをお履きになって
　　　　　　窓からお離れに
　　　　　　ミルクとクラッカーです
アン　　：健康によいことばかりね
夫人　　：よく眠れますよ
アン　　：疲れすぎて眠れそうにないわ

CTS : Now, my dear, if you don't mind, tomorrow's schedule — or "schedule" — whichever you prefer. Both are correct. 8:30, breakfast here with the Embassy staff.
Nine o'clock we leave for the Polinari Automotive Works, where you'll be presented with a small car.
ANN : "Thank you."
CTS : Which you will not accept.
ANN : "No, thank you."
CTS : 10:35, inspection of the Food and Agricultural Organization, which will present you with an olive tree.
ANN : "No, thank you."
CTS : Which you will accept.
ANN : "Thank you."
CTS : 10:55, the New Foundling Home for Orphans. You will preside over the laying of the cornerstone, same speech as last Monday.
ANN : Trade relations.
CTS : Yes.
ANN : For the orphans?
CTS : Oh, no, no, the other one.
ANN : Youth and progress.
CTS : Precisely. 11:45, back here to rest.
No, that's wrong, 11:45, conference here with the press.
ANN : Sweetness and decency.
CTS : One o'clock sharp, lunch with the Foreign Ministry. You will wear your white lace and carry a bouquet of —

夫人　　：明日の日程を
　　　　　"スケジュール"と言っても
　　　　　構いませんが
　　　　　8時30分 大使館員と朝食

　　　　　9時 ポリナリ自動車工場で
　　　　　小型車の贈呈があります
アン　　：感謝します
夫人　　：辞退あそばせ
アン　　：せっかくですが
夫人　　：10時35分 農業団体の視察
　　　　　オリーブの木が贈られます

アン　　：せっかくですが
夫人　　：お受けあそばせ
アン　　：感謝します
夫人　　：続いて10時55分
　　　　　孤児院の定礎式
　　　　　この前と同じスピーチを
アン　　：貿易の時と？
夫人　　：そうです
アン　　：孤児に対して？
夫人　　：いいえ 違うほう
アン　　："若者と進歩"
夫人　　：それです　11時45分
　　　　　一時休憩
　　　　　違いました　ここで記者会見
アン　　："優しさと品格"ね
夫人　　：1時 外交官との昼食会
　　　　　白いレースのドレスに

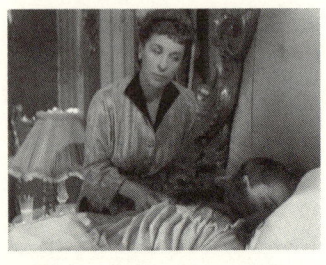

Please let me die in peace!
「安らかに死なせて！」

ANN : very small pink roses.
CTS : 3:05, presentation of a plaque.
ANN : "Thank you."
CTS : 4:10, review special guard of Carabiniere Police.
ANN : "No, thank you."
CTS : 4:45...
ANN : "How do you do?"
CTS : back here to change...
ANN : "Charmed."
CTS : to your uniform...
ANN : "So happy."
CTS : to meet the international ar...
ANN : Stop!!
CTS : Could you...
ANN : Stop, stop, stop!
CTS : It's all right, dear, it didn't spill.
ANN : I don't care if it's spilled or not!
I don't care if I drown in it!

I'll be dead before he gets here.

「来るころには
死んでいるから」

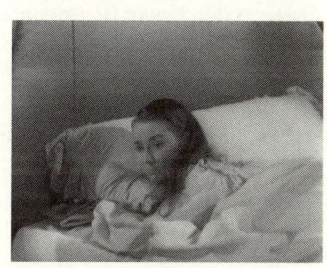

アン	：ピンクのバラのブーケ
夫人	：3時5分 額の授与
(アン	：感謝します)
夫人	：4時10分 騎銃警察隊の閲兵
(アン	：せっかくですが)
(夫人	：4時45分…)
アン	：はじめまして
(夫人	：戻られて…)
アン	：お会いできて光栄です
(夫人	：礼装に)
(アン	：光栄です)
(夫人	：国際…)
アン	：やめて！
(夫人	：王女様…)
アン	：やめてったら！
夫人	：こぼれてなかった
アン	：そんなのどうでもいいわ （その中で溺れてもいい！）

CTS : My dear, you're ill!
　　　　I'll send for Dr. Bonnachoven.
ANN : I don't want Dr. Bonnachoven.
　　　　Please let me die in peace!
CTS : You're not dying!
ANN : Leave me! Leave me!
CTS : It's nerves! Control yourself, Ann!
ANN : I don't want to!
CTS : Your Highness!
　　　　I'll get Dr. Bonnachoven.
ANN : It's no use.
　　　　I'll be dead before he gets here.

このセリフ、会話にいただき！
- **I'm not two hundred years old.**「私は200歳ではない」とかなり大げさだが、「私は年寄りではない」という意味の表現。そうめずらしくはないので、ユーモアを交えて「自分はまだ若い」と言いたいときに使える。

このニュアンスを味わう！
- **Your milk and crackers.** は欧米では子どもが寝る前にミルクを飲ませる習慣があることから。これはアン王女がまだ子供っぽいことを表現している。大人の女性に成長する前の重要な伏線。

夫人　：まあ ご病気ですね
　　　　お医者様を呼ぶわ
アン　：要らない
　　　　安らかに死なせて
夫人　：死にませんよ
アン　：ほっておいて
夫人　：お気を静めて
アン　：イヤよ！
夫人　：王女様
　　　　医者を呼びます
アン　：そんなのムダよ
　　　　来るころには死んでるから

このセリフ、会話にいただき！

- **Precisely** は **exactly** と同じで「まさにそのとおり」と相手の言ったことに対して肯定する表現。1語だけでもいいが、**That's precisely what I meant.**（まさに私が言いたかったことです）のように使える。
- **One o'clock sharp** の **sharp** は「きっかり」の意味。**I'll meet you there at one o'clock sharp.**（そこで1時きっかりに会おう）のように使える。**One o'clock precisely.** とも言える。

Scene 4 　大使館・アン王女の寝室
「医師の注射」

There she goes again.
「ほら、またですわ」

DOC : She is asleep.
CTS : She was in hysterics three minutes ago, Doctor.
DOC : Are you asleep, Ma'am?
ANN : No!
DOC : Oh! I'll only disturb Your Royal Highness a moment, ah?
ANN : I'm very ashamed, Dr. Bonnachoven. I...suddenly I was crying.
DOC : Humph. To cry — perfectly normal thing to do.
GEN : It's most important she be calm and relaxed for the press conference, Doctor.
ANN : Don't worry, Doctor.
　　　I — I'll be calm and relaxed and I - I'll bow and I'll smile and — I'll improve trade relations and I, and I will...
CTS : There she goes again. Give her something, Doctor, please!
DOC : Uncover her arm, please, hmm?
ANN : What's that?

Can I keep just one light on?

「明かりをひとつ
　つけたままでも？」

医者　：眠ってる
夫人　：3分前まではヒステリーを
医者　：お休みで？
アン　：全然
医者　：少々 失礼いたしますよ

アン　：先生 私 恥ずかしいですわ
　　　　急に泣いたりして
医者　：泣くのは自然なことです
将軍　：記者会見には
　　　　落ち着いてご出席を
アン　：大丈夫よ
　　　　もうすぐ落ち着くから
　　　　にっこり笑ってお辞儀をして
　　　　貿易関係の促進…
夫人　：まただわ
　　　　注射をお願いします
医者　：袖をまくって
アン　：何なの？

DOC : Sleep and calm.
This will relax you and make Your Highness feel a little happy.
It's a new drug, quite harmless. There.
ANN : I don't feel any different.
DOC : You will. It may take a little time to take hold. Just now, lie back, huh?
ANN : Can I keep just one light on?
DOC : Of course. Best thing I know is to do exactly what you wish for a while.
ANN : Thank you, Doctor.
CTS : Oh, the General! Doctor, quick!
DOC : Oh!
ANN : Hah!
GEN : I'm perfectly all right!
Good night, Ma'am.
DOC : Good night, Ma'am.
ANN : Good night, Doctor.

このセリフ、会話にいただき！
- **I'm very ashamed.**（とても恥ずかしいわ）は、恥を重んじる日本人に適した表現。**You have nothing to be ashamed of.**（あなたは何も恥ずかしいことはしていない）のように使える。
- **There she goes again.**（彼女またやってる）は、よくないことを繰り返す相手に対する非難の表現。**There you go again, Irving!**（またやってるよ、アービング！）とジョーも使っている（188ページ）。

医者	：安定剤 お気持ちが楽になり いいご気分に 新薬ですよ　ほらね
アン	：効果なしよ
医者	：少し経てば効いてくるでしょう 今は横になって
アン	：電気をつけたままでも？
医者	：もちろんです 今は できるだけお好きなように
アン	：ありがとう
夫人	：まあ将軍が　急いで
(医者	：おお)
(アン	：まあ)
将軍	：私なら大丈夫 お休みなさい
医者	：お休みなさいませ
アン	：お休みなさい

このセリフ、会話にいただき！

- **Can I keep just one light on?**（明かりを 1 つだけつけててもいいかしら？）の **Can I...?** は家族や親しい人に気楽な感じで許可を求める表現。**Can I come in?**（入ってもいい？）のように使える。
- **I'm perfectly all right!** は「私はまったく大丈夫です！」と強調したいときに使える。

Scene 5

ホテルの一室
「記者仲間のポーカー」

I gotta get up early.

「早く起きなきゃならないんだ」

CSH : Bet five hundred.
JOE : Five hundred. How many?
IRV : One.
CSH : I'll take one.
MAN : Three.
JOE : Four...boy! Two for papa.
CSH : Five hundred more.
JOE : Without looking.
IRV : Five hundred – and...uh I'll raise you a thousand.
CSH : Two pairs.
JOE : Oh, well, I've got three shy little sevens.
IRV : Er, a nervous straight.
　　　Come home, you fools.
　　　Now, look at that: six thousand five hundred – ah, not bad, that's ten bucks.
　　　Er, one more round and I'm going to throw you gents right out in the snow.
　　　I got to get up early.

Well, it works out fine for me.
「僕には好都合だ」

キャシ　：500リラ
ジョー　：何枚要る？
アビン　：1枚
キャシ　：俺も1枚
男　　　：3枚くれ
ジョー　：4枚　親に2枚
キャシ　：さらに500
ジョー　：乗った
アビン　：500だ　そしてさらに1000賭ける
キャシ　：ツーペア
ジョー　：慎ましく7のスリーカード
アビン　：こっちはストレート
　　　　　みんな戻っておいで
　　　　　6500リラなら10ドルか
　　　　　悪くないな
　　　　　あと1回やったら
　　　　　みんな帰ってもらおう
　　　　　朝が早いんだよ

IRV : Date with Her Royal Highness, who will graciously pose for some pictures.
JOE : What do you mean 'early'?
My personal invitation says 11:45.
CSH : Couldn't be anything to do with the fact that you're ahead?
IRV : It could.
JOE : Well, it works out fine for me.
This is my last five thousand.
And you hyenas are not going to get it.
Thanks a lot, Irving.
IRV : Yeah.
JOE : See you at Annie's little party in the morning.
IRV : Ciao, Joe.
JOE : Yep, ciao.
ALL : Goodbye, Goodnight, Joe.
JOE : Ciao. Stay sober.
IRV : All right, a little seven card stud.
CSH : Okay with me.

このセリフ、会話にいただき！
- **Bet five hundred.** の **bet** はその本来の意味で「賭ける」だが、(お金を賭けるほど)「確かだ、確信する」という意味もある。**I bet you had a good time.** と言えば「きっと楽しかったことでしょうね」。

このニュアンスを味わう！
- **Come home.** は賭け事でよく使う表現で、**fools** は「お金」のこと。**buck** は米俗語で「ドル」。**buckskin**（鹿の皮）が語源で18世紀に商売・取引の単位だった。19世紀になって「ドル」を表すようになった。

アビン　：王女様のお写真を
　　　　　撮りに行く
ジョー　：早いって？
　　　　　確か招待は11時45分のはずだ
キャシ　：勝ち逃げする気か？

アビン　：かもね
ジョー　：（僕には好都合）
　　　　　もう5000リラしかない
　　　　　巻き上げられる前に帰る
　　　　　（どうもな　アービング）
（アビン：ああ）
ジョー　：それじゃ 明朝　王女のパーティーで
アビン　：またな ジョー
（ジョー：じゃあ）
（**全員**　：お休み、ジョー）
（ジョー：あまり飲むな）
アビン　：セブンカード・スタッドでやろう
（キャシ：乗った）

このニュアンスを味わう！
● throw you gents right out in the snow. は「君たちを雪のまっただ中に投げ込む」→「君たちを外に追い出す」→「帰ってもらう」。

このセリフ、会話にいただき！
● What do you mean 'early'? ("早い"ってどういう意味?) は、'early' を変えるだけでいろいろと質問できる。What do you mean 'organic'? ("有機"ってどういう意味?) など。What do you mean by that? と言ってもいい。
● It works out fine for me. は「私にとって都合がいい」と言いたいときに使える。work out fine は「ちょうどよくなる」。

Scene 6　フォロ・ロマーノ
「ジョーとアン王女の初めての出会い」

Whadya know! You're well-read, well-dressed...
「こりゃ驚いた！ 教養があって、身なりもいい…」

ANN : Sooooo...happy... How're are you this evening?
　　　Mmmmmmmm...hmmmmm...mmmmmmmmm...
JOE : Hey – hey – hey – hey!
　　　Hey, wake up! Wake up.
ANN : Thank you very much. Delighted.
　　　No, thank you... Charmed...
JOE : Charmed, too.
ANN : You may sit down.
JOE : I think you'd better sit up.
　　　Much too young to get picked up by the police.
ANN : Police?
JOE : Yep, po-lice.
ANN : 2:15 and back here to change. 2:45...
JOE : You know, people who can't handle liquor
　　　shouldn't drink it.
ANN : "If I were dead and buried and I heard your voice
　　　- beneath the sod my heart of dust would still
　　　rejoice." Do you know that poem?
JOE : Huh! What do you know!

All right.
I'll drop you
off, come on.
「じゃ、送ってやるよ、さあ」

アン　　：光栄…です…
　　　　　　今夜のご気分は？
ジョー　：ちょっとお嬢さん
　　　　　　起きて
アン　　：ありがたく嬉しく
　　　　　　光栄ですわ
ジョー　：こちらこそ
アン　　：掛けなさい
ジョー　：起きなきゃ警察に
　　　　　　しょっぴかれるぞ
アン　　：警察に？
（ジョー：そう　警察だ）
アン　　：2時15分　戻って着替え　2時45分…
ジョー　：いいかい
　　　　　　酒に弱い人は飲んではいけない
アン　　："死して埋められるとも君が声を聞かば
　　　　　　土の下に眠るわが心は喜びに満ちるであろう"
　　　　　　この詩をご存じ？
ジョー　：こりゃ驚いた！

JOE : You're well-read, well-dressed...snoozing away in a public street.
Would you care to make a statement?
ANN : What the world needs is a return to sweetness and decency in the souls of its young men and... mmmmmhhhhhhhmmmmm...
JOE : Yeah, I...uh...couldn't agree with you more, but um... Get yourself some coffee, you'll be all right. Look, you take the cab.
ANN : Mmmmm.
JOE : Come on, climb in the cab and go home.
ANN : Mmmmm...mmmmmm, so happy.
JOE : You got any money?
ANN : Never carry money.
JOE : That's a bad habit.
ANN : Mm.
JOE : All right. I'll drop you off, come on.
ANN : It's a taxi!
JOE : Well, it's not the Super Chief.

このニュアンスを味わう!

- **You may sit down.**(座ってもよろしい)の **may** は上の者が下の者に「許可を与える」というニュアンスなので使い方に注意。**May I come in?**(入ってもよろしいでしょうか?)と自分に使うときは非常にていねい。

- **Much too young to get picked up by the police.** には「かなり若いのに警察につかまったら困るだろう」というニュアンスがある。「**get**＋過去分詞」には「やられて困る」という含みがある。

- **People who can't handle liquor shouldn't drink it.** は一般論で柔らかいニュアンス。直接アンを非難せず間接的で心優しいジョーの一面が表れている。

ジョー	: 学もあって身なりもいいのに
	道で寝ているとはね
	何かご意見があれば
アン	: 世界に必要なのは
	若者たちの心に優しさと
	品格を取り戻すことです
ジョー	: ごもっともだけど
	コーヒーを飲めば良くなる
	君が乗りなさい
(アン	: う〜ん)
ジョー	: タクシーで家に帰るんだ
アン	: 光栄です
ジョー	: 金はある？
アン	: 持ち歩かないの
ジョー	: 悪い癖だな
(アン	: そう)
ジョー	: 送ってやるよ
アン	: タクシーだわ
ジョー	: 高級車じゃないけど

このニュアンスを味わう!

● snoozing away で「平気で眠りこけている」というニュアンス。snoozing は sleeping よりかなりくだけた態度を示す。away で「平気でやっている」感じが追加される。

● I couldn't agree with you more. は「完全に同意していて、これ以上は同意しようがない」という意味で I agree with you completely. と同じ。「まさにその通り」か「大賛成」。

● the Super Chief は当時の高級車 the Star Chief のもじり。Well, it's not the Super Chief. は「高級車じゃないけどね」といった感じ。

Scene 7 タクシー
「タクシーの行き先」

Look, now where do you wanna go?
「おい、さあどこに行きたいんだ？」

DRV : Dove andiamo?
　　　Where're we going?
JOE : Where do you live?
ANN : Mmmmmm? Colosseum.
JOE : Now, come on, you're not that drunk.
ANN : You're so smart – I'm not drunk at all.
　　　I'm just being verrrrry haaaappy......
JOE : Hey, now, don't fall asleep again. Come on.
DRV : Per favore, signore – ho detto dove andiamo?
　　　Where are we – we going?
JOE : Lo diro in un momento dove fermare.
DRV : Okay.
JOE : Look, now where do you want to go? Hmmm?
　　　Where shall I take you?
　　　Where do – where do - where do you live?
　　　Huh? Huh? Come on.
　　　Come on, where do you live?
ANN : Uhh-umm...
JOE : Come on – where do you live?

Come on – where do you live?
「さあ、どこに住んでる?」
I...ohhhhh... Colosseum.
「私…うーん…コロセウム」

運転手 : どこへ行きますかい?

ジョー : 家はどこだ?
アン　 : コロセウム
ジョー : 酔ったふりは よせ
アン　 : 鋭いわね　私は酔ってない
　　　　 ただ気分がいいだけよ
ジョー : おい　寝るんじゃない
運転手 : どこへ行けばいいんです?

ジョー : 少し待ってくれ　行き先を言うから
(運転手 : へい)
ジョー : どこまで送ればいい?
　　　　 家はどこにある?
　　　　 言えよ
　　　　 どこに住んでるんだ

(アン　 : う〜ん…)
ジョー : 家はどこだ?

ANN : I...ohhhhh...Colosseum.
JOE : She lives in the Colosseum.
DRV : Is wrong address.
Now, look, segnore, for me it is very late night and mia moglie – my wife... I have three bambino – three bambino, ah – you know, bambino? My- my taxi go home, I – I go home er too, together, signore... Excuse me.
JOE : Via Margutta 51.
DRV : Via Margutta 51.
Oh, molto bene!

このイタリア語がわかればもっと楽しめる！
● **Dove andiamo?** は英語の直訳では Where we go? タクシーの運転手はその後に Where're we going? と英語で同じ意味のことを言っている。

このセリフ、会話にいただき！
● このシーンでジョーは何度も come on と言っているが、「さあさあ」「だめだ」のほかにも「おいで」「急いで」「やってごらん」といった意味で使える。**Come on, we're going to be late.**（早く、遅れるよ）など。

アン	：コロセウム
ジョー	：コロセウムだとさ
運転手	：それは おかしい
	だんな もう夜も遅い
	うちでは妻と
	3人の子供が待ってる
	タクシーは家に帰る
	私も一緒に家に帰る
ジョー	：マルグッタ通り51へ
運転手	：マルグッタ通り51か
	よしきた

このトリビアで通になろう！
● **Roman Holiday** とは本来「他人を苦しめて得る娯楽」の意味。古代ローマ人の娯楽とアン王女のつかの間のアバンチュールをかけたタイトル。その象徴が **Colosseum** でアン王女が自分の住まいだと言うのが面白い。

このイタリア語がわかればもっと楽しめる！
● イタリア語ではふつう主語が省略されるため運転手は Is wrong address. と It を省略。mia moglie は my wife、bambino は child、molto bene は very good。

Scene 8 マルグッタ通り・ジョーのアパートの前
「運転手とのやり取り」

Take her wherever she wants to go.
「この娘が行きたい所に行ってくれ」

DRV : Here is Via Margutta 51 – Cinquantuno.
I am very happy.
Thousand lira - mille lire.
JOE : Mille. Cinquemila.
DRV : One – two – three – four mila.
JOE : Okay. Mille per te.
DRV : For me?
JOE : Si.
DRV : Oh, grazie mille.
JOE : Okay – okay. Look – take a little bit of that ...
DRV : Aah...
JOE : Take her wherever she wants to go.
DRV : Aah-haah.
JOE : Huh? Capito? Capito.
Huh-ha, buona notte.
DRV : Good night. Buona notte. Oh! No, no, momento, momento, momento! No, no, no. No, no, no.
JOE : All right, all right. Look, as soon as she wakes up, see?

Look, look, pal, this is not my problem, see?

「いいかい、いいかい、君、僕の問題じゃないんだ、分かる?」

運転手 ：マルグッタ通り51ね
　　　　いや よかった
　　　　1000リラです
ジョー ：5000リラだ
運転手 ：4000リラのお釣り
ジョー ：チップだ
運転手 ：あっしに?
(ジョー：そう)
運転手 ：どうも
ジョー ：それで少し頼まれてくれないか
(運転手：はぁ)
ジョー ：この娘が行きたい所に行ってくれ　いいな?
(運転手：はぁ)
(ジョー：分かったかい?
　　　　じゃお休み)
運転手 ：お休み
　　　　ちょいと待った (ダメダメ)
(ジョー：分かったよ 目が覚めたらだ)

DRV : Yeah...
JOE : She tell you where she want to go. Okay.
DRV : Momento, momento.
　　　My taxi is not for sleep, my taxi, no sleep.
　　　You understand? You understand?
JOE : Look, look, pal, this is not my problem, see?
　　　I never see her before. Huh? Okay.
DRV : Is not your problem, is not my problem.
　　　What you want? You don't want girl, yeah?
　　　Me don't want girl. Police!
　　　Maybe she want girl!
JOE : Stay calmo, stay calmo. Okay, okay, okay.
　　　Va bene, va bene.

アパート・中庭
「眠りたいアン王女」

ANN : So happy. So happy.

このニュアンスを味わう！
● **take a little bit of that** は「そこから少し取って」の意味。1000リラを余計に渡して運転手にアンを送ってもらうつもり。1000リラは当時で約1.5ドル、現在では17ドル。

このイタリア語がわかればもっと楽しめる！
● **Cinquantuno** は51で、**Cinquemila** は5000リラ。**Mille per te.** は **Mille for you.** のこと。**Grazie mille.** は **Thanks a lot.**（どうもありがとう）で **Capito?** は **Understood?**（わかった）。**Buona notte** は **Good night**（おやすみ）。

運転手　：へい
ジョー　：いいかい　起きたら行き先を言うはずだ
運転手　：ちょいと
　　　　　タクシーは寝る所じゃない
　　　　　お分かり？
ジョー　：いいかい　この娘とは
　　　　　初めて会ったばかりだ
運転手　：あっしだって関係ない
　　　　　あんたは娘 要らない
　　　　　あっしも娘 要らない
　　　　　たぶん 警察は娘 要るかも
ジョー　：分かったよ
　　　　　騒ぐんじゃない

アン　　：光栄です　嬉しく思います

このニュアンスを味わう！
- She tell you where she want to go. や I never see her before. は文法的には誤りだが、ジョーはイタリア人運転手に伝わるようにあえて動詞の原型を使って話している。

このイタリア語がわかればもっと楽しめる！
- Police! Maybe she want girl!では、イタリア語で「警察」は女性名詞なので she を使っている。
- Stay calm.（落ち着け）のイタリア語は Stai calmo. でジョーは Stay calmo. と混ぜこぜにしている。Va bene は直訳では Goes well で、ここでは Okay の意味。

47

Scene 9

ジョーのアパート・室内
「ジョーとアン王女とパジャマ」

Is this the elevator?
「これはエレベーター？」
It's my room!
「僕の部屋だよ！」

JOE : Out of my head.
ANN : Is this the elevator?
JOE : It's my room!
ANN : I'm terribly sorry to mention it, but the dizziness is getting worse.
Can I sleep here?
JOE : That's the general idea.
ANN : Can I have a silk nightgown with rosebuds on it?
JOE : I'm afraid you'll have to rough it tonight - in these.
ANN : Pajamas!
JOE : Sorry, honey, but I haven't worn a nightgown in years.
ANN : Will you help me get undressed, please?
JOE : Er...okay. Er, there you are.
You can handle the rest.
ANN : May I have some?
JOE : No! Now look...

Will you help me get undressed, please?
「脱ぐのを手伝って
　くださる？」

Er...okay.
「その…いいよ」

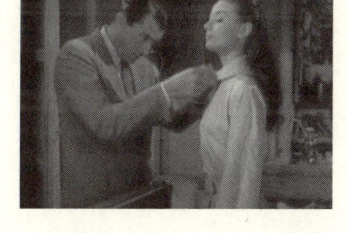

ジョー　　：どうかしてるよ
アン　　　：これはエレベーター？
ジョー　　：僕の部屋だよ
アン　　　：申し上げにくいのですが
　　　　　　めまいがひどくなりました
　　　　　　ここで寝ても？
ジョー　　：しかたがないね
アン　　　：バラの刺しゅうがついたシルクのネグリジェは？
ジョー　　：これで我慢してくれ
　　　　　　これで
アン　　　：パジャマだわ
ジョー　　：何年もナイトガウンは着てない

アン　　　：脱ぐのを手伝ってくださる？
ジョー　　：オーケー
　　　　　　後は自分で
アン　　　：私もいただける？
ジョー　　：ダメだ　いいか

I've never been alone with a man before...

「これまで殿方と2人きりになったことはありません…」

ANN : This is very unusual.
I've never been alone with a man before, even with my dress on.
With my dress off, it's most unusual.
Hm, I don't seem to mind. Do you?
JOE : I think I'll go out for a cup of coffee.
ANN : Hm.
JOE : You'd better get to sleep.
ANN : Hm?
JOE : Oh, no – no. On this one.
ANN : So terribly nice.
JOE : Hey – hey, come here.
These are pajamas.
They're to sleep in.
You're to climb into them.
You understand?
ANN : Thank you.
JOE : And you do your sleeping on the couch, see?

...on the couch. Is that clear?

「…長椅子の上だ。
　分かったな？」

アン　　：とても珍しいことだわ
　　　　　男の人と2人きりは初めて
　　　　　たとえ服を着てても
　　　　　それが服を脱ぐだなんて
　　　　　でも気にならないの　あなたは？
ジョー　：コーヒーを飲んでくる
(アン　　：う〜ん)
ジョー　：君は　もう寝なさい
(アン　　：え？)
ジョー　：ここじゃない　あっちだ
アン　　：まあ　ご親切に
ジョー　：さっさと
　　　　　このパジャマを着て寝るんだ
　　　　　分かった？

(アン　　：感謝します)
ジョー　：君が寝る場所は長椅子だ

JOE : Not on the bed, not on the chair, on the couch. Is that clear?
ANN : Do you know my favorite poem?
JOE : Ah, you've already recited that for me.
ANN : Arethusa arose, from her couch of snows, in the Akraceronian Mountains. Keats.
JOE : Shelley.
ANN : Keats!
JOE : You just keep your mind off the poetry and on the pajamas, everything will be all right, see?
ANN : It's Keats.
JOE : I'll be – it's Shelley – I'll be back in about ten minutes.
ANN : Keats. You have my permission – to withdraw.
JOE : Thank you very much.

このセリフの発音に注意！
- 脚本を調べると I ought to have my head examined.（頭ん中を調べなきゃ）となっているが、ジョーは Out of my head.（頭がおかしい／気が狂っている）のように発音。I oughta've my head... と言って最後が聞こえないのかも。

このニュアンスを味わう！
- That's the general idea. は「そう考えるのがふつう」という意味。general idea は「一般的な考え」や「一般概念」。

ジョー	：ベッドじゃない
	いいな？
アン	：私の好きな詩を？
ジョー	：もうさっき聞いた
アン	："雪の長椅子よりアレトゥサは立ち上がる
	アクロサロニアの山々に抱かれて" キーツよ
ジョー	：シェリーだ
アン	：キーツよ
ジョー	：詩は いいからパジャマを着ろ
	楽になる
アン	：キーツよ
ジョー	：シェリーだよ
	10分ほどで戻る
アン	：もう下がってよろしい
ジョー	：そりゃ どうも

このニュアンスを味わう！
- I've never been alone with a man before... は、アンはまだ男性経験がないことを知らせる重要なセリフ。今後の展開の重要な伏線。
- ジョーが「couch（長椅子）の上で寝るんだ」と言うと、アンは「couch of snows（雪の長椅子）から立ち上がる」と詩で答えるところが面白い。

このトリビアで通になろう！
- この詩「Arethusa」の作者をアンは Keats と勘違いしており、ジョーが言う Shelley が正しい。2人とも19世紀イギリス・ロマン派を代表する詩人で、「キーツ・シェリー博物館」がスペイン階段の右手にある。

Scene 10　大使館・大使の書斎
「アン王女の失踪」

Have you searched the grounds?
「敷地内も捜したか？」

AMB : Well?
OFF : No trace, Your Excellency.
AMB : Have you searched the grounds?
OFF : Every inch, Sir, from the attics to the cellar.
AMB : I must put you on your honor not to speak of this to anyone.
　　　 I must remind you that the Princess is the direct heir to the throne.
　　　 This must be classified as top-crisis secret.
　　　 Have I your pledge?
OFF : Yes, Sir.
AMB : Very well.
　　　 Now we must notify Their Majesties.

このニュアンスを味わう！
- このシーンで大使は強制的な must を4度も使っている。must の核となる意味は「〜しなければならない」という義務感。自分には「義務」、相手には「命令」や「説教」となる。

This must be classified as top-crisis secret.

「この件は最高機密扱いだ」

大使	:それで？
職員	:どこにも
大使	:庭も捜した？
職員	:屋根裏から地下室まで
大使	:この件について他言は無用
	王女は第一の王位継承者であられる
	これは最重要機密だ
	他言しないと誓うか？
(職員	:はい)
大使	:よろしい
	では両陛下にご報告しなければ

このセリフ、会話にいただき！
- **Well?** はここでは「それで？」の意味。
- **Have I your pledge?** は相手に「誓うか？」とたずねる表現。**I'll take a pledge.** と言えば自分が誓うこと。

Scene 11 ジョーのアパート・室内
「ジョーの寝過ごし」

"大使館より緊急配信
アン王女が突然の発病"

JOE : Huh? Oh!
ANN : So happy.
JOE : The pleasure is mine.
　　　Screwball!

JOE : Holy smoke, the Princess' interview!
ANN : Uh?
JOE : Eleven forty-five!
ANN : Uhnnn...
JOE : Oh, shhh...!

このセリフ、会話にいただき！
● **The pleasure is mine.** は本来は心がこもった「どういたしまして」だが、ジョーは反対の気持ちを込めている。この表現は **My pleasure.** だけでもいいし、フォーマルなら **You're welcome.** で、カジュアルなら **Sure.** と言う。

Holy smoke...
「これは大変…」

アン   ：嬉しく思います
ジョー ：どういたしまして
　　　　　変な女

ジョー ：しまった　王女の記者会見が

ジョー ：11時45分だっけ

ジョー ：何てこった

このニュアンスを味わう！
- Screwball は「奇人・変人」の意味。Holy smoke. は Oh, my God.（これは大変）と同じ。他に Holy cow. やHoly shit. などの表現がある。

Scene 12 アメリカン・ニュース社のオフィス
「ジョーの遅刻」

"アメリカン・ニュース
アン王女 急病のため
記者会見は中止"

STF : Hi, Joe.
SEC : Good morning, Joe.
JOE : Hello, honey.
SEC : Mr. Hennessy has been looking for you.
JOE : Uh-oh. Thanks a lot, hon.

HEN :   Come in.

このニュアンスを味わう！
- 秘書から Mr. Hennessy has been looking for you. と言われてジョーは Uh-oh。このイントネーションに注意。「これはマズイぞ」というニュアンス。
- Thanks a lot, hon. の hon は honey の略。ふつうは妻や恋人への呼びかけだが、ここでは秘書に親しみを込めて呼びかけている。

Mr. Hennessy has been looking for you.
「支局長が捜してたわ」

記者	：よう ジョー
秘書	：おはようございます
ジョー	：やあ どうも
秘書	：支局長が捜してたわ
ジョー	：まずいな ありがとう
支局長	：入りたまえ

このニュアンスを味わう！
- ジョーが秘書のサンドイッチをほうばるのは、64ページで **Certainly pretty hard to swallow.**（呑み込みかねます）と言わせるための伏線。

Scene 13 ヘネシーのオフィス
「ジョーの言い訳と支局長の追及」

I've got 'em right here, somewhere.
「ちょうどここに、どこかに ありますよ」

JOE : You've been looking for me?
HEN : Just coming to work?
JOE : Who, me?
HEN : We start our days at 8:30 in this office!
We pick up our assignments...
JOE : I picked up mine last night.
HEN : What assignment was that?
JOE : The Princess – 11:45.
HEN : You've already been to the interview?
JOE : Why, sure. I just got back.
HEN : Well, well, well... All my apologies.
JOE : It's all right.
HEN : Er, this is very interesting.
JOE : Nah, just routine.
HEN : Tell me, tell me, did she answer all the questions on the list?
JOE : Well, of course she did.
I've got them right here, somewhere.

Yes, Mr. Bradley, in toto.
「そう、ブラッドレー君 すべてだ」

Certainly pretty hard to swallow.
「呑み込みかねます」

ジョー　　：お捜しで？
支局長　　：今ごろ 出社か
ジョー　　：まさか
支局長　　：わが社は8時半始業だ
　　　　　　割り当てを…
ジョー　　：昨夜 もらいました
支局長　　：何の仕事だ？
ジョー　　：王女の記者会見
支局長　　：それに行ってきたのか？
ジョー　　：その戻りですよ
支局長　　：なるほど　それは悪かったな
（ジョー　：いいえ）
支局長　　：これは面白い
ジョー　　：いつものことですよ
支局長　　：質問には全部 答えたか？

ジョー　　：もちろん
　　　　　　どこかにありますよ

HEN : Ah, don't disturb yourself — I have a copy here.
How did Her Highness react to the idea of a European Federation?
JOE : She thought it was just fine.
HEN : She did?
JOE : Well, she thought that there'd be...two effects.
HEN : Two?
JOE : The er, direct and the...indirect.
HEN : Oh, remarkable.
JOE : Naturally, she thought that the indirect would not be as...direct...as the direct.
That is, not right away.
HEN : No, no, no, no, no.
JOE : Later on, of course, well, nobody knows.
HEN : Well, well, well.
That was a shrewd observation!
They fool you, you know, these royal kids.
They've got a lot more on the ball than we suspect.
How did she feel about the future friendship of nations?
JOE : Youth.
HEN : Yep?
JOE : She felt that, er, the youth of the world must lead the way to a better...world.
HEN : Hmm-hmm. Original. Er, by the way, what was she wearing?
JOE : Oh, you mean what did she have on?
HEN : Well, that's usually what it means.
Er, what's the matter, is it a little warm in here for you?

支局長　：いや 結構　ここに写しがある
　　　　　欧州連邦化について
　　　　　何と答えていた？
ジョー　："賛成です"と
支局長　：本当に？
ジョー　：2つの効果が見込めると
(支局長：2つ？)
ジョー　：直接的と間接的な効果が
支局長　：注目の発言だ
ジョー　：当然ながら間接効果は
　　　　　直接効果ほど直接的でなく即効性はないと
　　　　　そのうちに
(支局長：そう　そうだね)
ジョー　：でも先のことはね
支局長　：なるほど
　　　　　鋭い洞察力だな
　　　　　王室は人をからかうよ
　　　　　意外と頭がいいな

　　　　　今後の諸国間の親交については？

ジョー　：若者です
(支局長：そう？)
ジョー　："世界の若者が先頭に立って
　　　　　より良い世界を作るべき"そう 王女はお考えです
支局長　：独創的だ
　　　　　ところで服装は？
ジョー　：つまり何を着てたか？
支局長　：それ以外の意味があるか？
　　　　　ここは暑いか？

JOE : No, no. I just hurried over here.
HEN : Oh, naturally, with a story of these dimensions. Did you say she was wearing gray?
JOE : No, I didn't say that.
HEN : Well, she usually wears gray.
JOE : Oh, well, er, it was a...kind of a gray.
HEN : Oh, I think I know the dress you mean. It has a gold collar around the neck.
JOE : That's the one, that's the one. Yeah, I didn't know exactly how to describe it but that's it, yeah.
HEN : I think you described it very well. In view of the fact that Her Highness was taken violently ill at three o'clock this morning, put to bed with a high fever, and has had all her appointments for today cancelled in toto!
JOE : In toto?
HEN : Yes, Mr. Bradley, in toto.
JOE : Certainly pretty hard to swallow.
HEN : In view of the fact that you just left her, of course. But here it is, Mr. Bradley, all over the front page of every newspaper in Rome!
JOE : All right, all right, I overslept. It can happen to anybody!
HEN : If you ever got up early enough to read a morning paper, you might discover little news events, little items of general interest that might prevent you in the future from getting enmeshed in such a gold-plated, triple-decked, star-spangled lie as you have just told me!

ジョー	：いえ 急いだので
支局長	：なんせ重要な記事だからな 　グレーの服だと言った？
ジョー	：言ってません
支局長	：いつもはそうだが
ジョー	：そういえばグレー系の色でしたね
支局長	：金の襟がついてるドレスか？
ジョー	：それですよ 　うまく説明できなくて
支局長	：うまい説明だったよ 　王女は未明3時にご発病 　高熱で床にふされ 　今日のご予定は 　すべて中止になったのに
ジョー	：すべて中止？
支局長	：そう ブラッドレー君　すべてだ
ジョー	：呑み込みかねます
支局長	：王女に会ったそうだからな 　ローマ中の新聞の 　一面を飾ってるぞ
ジョー	：確かに寝過ごしましたけど 　（誰にだってあること）
支局長	：普段から早起きして 　朝刊を読む癖があれば 　世間が注目する 　この記事にも気づいたはずだ 　すぐメッキのはがれるウソを 　つかずに済んだのに

HEN : If I were you, I would try some other line of business, like mattress testing!
JOE : Is this...the Princess?
HEN : Yes, Mr. Bradley!
That is the Princess.
It isn't Annie Oakley, Dorothy Lamour, or Madame Chiang Kai-shek.
Take a good look at her.
You might be interviewing her again some day!
JOE : Am I fired?
HEN : No, you're not fired.
When I want to fire you, you won't have to ask.
You'll know you're fired!
The man's mad!

オフィス入り口・電話
「ジョーの大家への依頼」

GIO : Pronto.
JOE : Giovanni, it's Joe Bradley.
Now, listen carefully.
I want you to hurry up to my place and see if there's somebody there, asleep.
GIO : Aha!
Si, Mr. Joe, I look subito, you wait – aspetta.

GIO : Mr. Joe?
JOE : Yeah! Er, yeah, yeah, yeah, tell me, tell me!
GIO : Bellissima!

支局長　：新しい職でも探したらどうだ

ジョー　：これが王女？
支局長　：そうだ ブラッドレー君

　　　　　　A・オークレーでも
　　　　　　D・ラムールでもない
　　　　　　よく拝んどけ
　　　　　　もう見れないかもな
ジョー　：つまりクビ？
支局長　：（クビじゃない）
　　　　　　クビにする時は聞く必要がないくらい
　　　　　　はっきり言ってやる
　　　　　　変なヤツめ

(ジョバ：もしもし)
ジョー　：ジョバンニか？　ジョーだ
　　　　　　よく聞いてくれ
　　　　　　急いで僕の部屋へ行き
　　　　　　誰かいるか見てくれ
ジョバ　：分かったよ
　　　　　　ジョーさん見てくるで お待ちを

ジョバ　：ジョーさん？
ジョー　：どうだった？
ジョバ　：べっぴんさんだ

67

JOE : Giovanni, I love you!
       Now, listen!
GIO : Yes, Mr. Joe – a gun? No!
JOE : Yes, a gun, a knife, anything!
       But nobody goes in and nobody goes out!
       Capito?
GIO : Okay.

このニュアンスを味わう！
- ジョーの You've been looking for me? は「ずっと探していたのですか？」という継続を表す。支局長のYou've already been to the interview? は「すでにインタビューに行ってきたのか？」という完了を表す。
- Well, well, well... は「それは、それは、それは」という意味。All my apologies. は「これはたいへん失礼」という感じ。フルセンテンスでは、Please accept my apologies.（ここにお詫びいたします）。
- They fool you は「人をかつぐ」。They've got a lot more on the ball は「かなり有能である」という意味。have a lot on the ball で「非常に有能だ」。
- in totoはラテン語で「すべて」や「完全に」という意味。in allや in the wholeと同じ。舞台がローマなのでイタリア語のもととなったラテン語を使っている。
- Annie Oakleyはテレビや映画「アニーよ銃をとれ」の人気主人公、Dorothy Lamourは女ターザンとしてスターになったセクシー女優、Madame Chiang Kai-shekは「蔣介石夫人」。いずれも当時有名な女性で、支局長はアン王女を知らないジョーを責めている。

ジョー　：でかしたぞ
　　　　　よく聞くんだ
ジョバ　：聞いてるでよ　鉄砲？　いかんな
ジョー　：鉄砲でもヤリでも何でもいい
　　　　　誰も部屋に出入りさせるな
　　　　　分かったか？
ジョバ　：分かった

このダブル・ミーニングでにやり！
- ジョーがサンドイッチをごくりと飲み込んだあと、Certainly pretty hard to swallow.（呑み込みかねます）と言っているのが面白い。swallow に gulp down（呑み込む）と understand（理解する）の2重の意味をもたせている。

このセリフ、会話にいただき！
- **Don't disturb yourself.** は「それにはおよびません」という意味。「おかまいなく」という感じで **Don't bother.** も使える。カジュアルなら **No bother.** でもいい。
- **Take a good look at her.**（彼女をよく見るんだ）のように口語では「動詞＋形容詞＋名詞」のパターンがよく使われる。英語のリズムがよくて言いやすいため。**Let me make a quick call.**（ちょっと電話させて）などと使える。

Scene 14 ヘネシーのオフィス
「ジョーと支局長の賭け」

> I know, but if I did, how much would it be worth?
> 「分かってますが、取れたらいくらです？」

HEN : You still here?
JOE : How much would a real interview with this dame be worth?
HEN : Are you referring to Her Highness?
JOE : I'm not referring to Annie Oakley, Dorothy Lamour, or Madame Chia... How much?
HEN : What do you care?
You've got about as much chance of getting...
JOE : I know, but if I did, how much would it be worth?
HEN : Oh, just a plain talk on world conditions, it might be worth two hundred and fifty.
Her views on clothes, of course, would be worth a lot more - maybe a thousand.
JOE : Dollars?
HEN : Dollars.
JOE : I'm talking about her views on everything.
HEN : Huh?

I want you to shake on 'at.
「約束の握手をしてください」

支局長　：まだ いたか
ジョー　：インタビューの価値は？

支局長　：王女の話か？
ジョー　：オークレーの話じゃなく
　　　　　さあ　いくらで？
支局長　：お前が聞いてどうする？
　　　　　（取れるわけないだろ…）
ジョー　：もし 取れたら？
支局長　：世界情勢についての
　　　　　コメントなら250
　　　　　ファッションの話なら
　　　　　1000ぐらい
ジョー　：ドルで？
（支局長：ドルだ）
ジョー　：あらゆる分野に関する話ならば？
（支局長：何？）

JOE : The private and secret longings of a princess...
her innermost thoughts as revealed to your Rome correspondent in a private, personal, exclusive interview.
Can't use it, huh?
I didn't think you'd like it.

HEN : Come here! Love angle too, I suppose?
JOE : Practically all love angle.
HEN : With pictures.
JOE : Could be. How much?
HEN : That particular story would be worth five grand to any news service.
But, er, tell me Mr. Bradley, if you are sober, just how you are going to obtain this fantastic interview?
JOE : I plan to enter her sickroom disguised as a thermometer. You said five grand? I want you to shake on that.
HEN : Ah, you realize, of course, Her Highness is in bed today and leaves for Athens tomorrow?
JOE : Yep.
HEN : Ah, now I'd like to make a little side bet with you. Five hundred says you don't come up with the story.
What are you looking at that for?
JOE : Oh, I just want to see what time it is.
HEN : Huh?
JOE : Er, what day it is, er – It's a deal!
HEN : Now I'd like you to shake.

ジョー　　：例えば"王女様の個人的で秘密の願い"
　　　　　　わが社の記者による独占インタビューで
　　　　　　密かな王女の心のうちを告白したら？

　　　　　　使えないか
　　　　　　支局長好みじゃないし

支局長　　：戻ってこい　恋の話もあるんだな？
ジョー　　：恋のいろんな面が
支局長　　：写真付きか？
ジョー　　：付くといくらに？
支局長　　：その記事なら
　　　　　　どこでも5000は出すだろう
　　　　　　その前に1つ聞かせてくれ
　　　　　　どうやって
　　　　　　インタビューを取る？
ジョー　　：体温計に変装して病室に入り込む
　　　　　　5000と言いましたね
　　　　　　では握手を
支局長　　：王女は明日にも
　　　　　　アテネに発つんだぞ
（ジョー　：分かってます）
支局長　　：じゃあ　私と賭けをしないか
　　　　　　記事が取れなければ500だ

　　　　　　どうして見てる？
ジョー　　：何時かと思いまして
（支局長　：え？）
ジョー　　：何曜日かと　　交渉成立
支局長　　：では約束の握手を

HEN : Let's see, you're into me for about five hundred now. When you lose this bet, you'll owe me a thousand.
Why, you poor sucker, I'll practically own you!
JOE : You have practically owned me for a couple of years now.
But that's all over.
I'm going to win that money and with it.
I'm going to buy me a one-way ticket back to New York!
HEN : Go on, go on.
I love to hear you whine!
JOE : And when I'm back in a real newsroom, I'll enjoy thinking about you, sitting here with an empty leash in your hands and nobody to twitch for you!
HEN : So long, pigeon.

このニュアンスを味わう!
- 支局長が Are you referring to Her Highness? と聞いたのに対して、ジョーは I'm not referring to Annie Oakley... と言い返して、1本取られたのを取り返している。
- a real newsroom は「地方に対する本物の編集室」のことで、ジョーは「本社の編集部」を意味している。
- sucker は「おめでたい人、だまされやすい人」で、pigeon は米俗語で「カモ、まぬけ、だまされやすい人」。英語では同じ意味の言葉を別の単語で表現する。

支局長	：今500貸してるから
	負けたら1000の貸しだ
	おめでたいな
	私の奴隷になるぞ
ジョー	：実質
	(数年間は)
	奴隷でしたが
	(それも終わり)
	今度は僕が勝ちます
	そしてニューヨークへ戻ります
支局長	：もっと言え
	お前の泣き言を聞きたい
ジョー	：本社で支局長のことを
	考えて楽しみますよ
	空の手綱を握って
	ここに座っている姿をね
支局長	：あばよ カモ君

このセリフ、会話にいただき！

- **What do you care?** は「何を心配している？」。care は「気遣う、心配する、案じる」という意味で、**I don't care.** なら「私は気にしない」。**Who cares?** は「誰がかまうものか？」。
- **grand** は1000ドルのことで、**five grand** は5000ドル。grand は **a grand sum of money**（大金）が1000ドルを意味したことが語源。ポピュラーになったのでGと略される。当時の5000ドルは現在の5万ドルくらい。
- **Five hundred says you don't come up with the story.** は「記事ができないほうに500ドルを賭ける」という意味で、**says** はこの場合は「賭ける」と理解する。

Scene 15

ジョーのアパート・中庭
「ジョーの借金話」

...absolutely nobody.
「全然誰も」

Swell! thanks a lot.
「すごい！ありがとう」

- GIO : Hup.
- KDS : All'assalto! All'assalto! Bang – bang!
- GIO : Fermi esagitati! – Basta!
  Se poi ragazzina si desta, ho montato la guardia fin ora.
- KDS : All'assalto!
- GIO : Via! Mascalzoni farabutti!
- JOE : Ciao, ragazzi.
- KDS : Hi, joe. Bongiorno signore.
- GIO : Signore Mr. Bradley.
  What's your problem?
- JOE : Everything okay, Giovanni?
- GIO : Listen here, Joe, uh, nobody has come, nobody has go, absolutely nobody.
- JOE : Swell! thanks a lot.
  Oh er, Giovanni, er... how would you like to make some money?
- GIO : Money?
- JOE : Yeah.

How would you like to make some money?

「金儲けをしたくはないかね?」

(ジョバ : いち・に)
子ども : 突撃! 突撃! バーン バーン!
ジョバ : やめろ
　　　　うるさいヤツらだ
　　　　あっちへ行け
子ども : 突撃!
ジョバ : あっちへ行け!悪ガキども!
ジョー : やあ みんな
子ども : こんにちわ
ジョバ : ブラッドレーさん
　　　　(どういうこと?)
ジョー : すべて順調か?
ジョバ : へえ この部屋には
　　　　誰も出入りしてないでな
ジョー : すごいな ありがとう
　　　　そうだ ジョバンニ
　　　　金儲けがしたくないか?
ジョバ : 金儲け?
(ジョー : そう)

GIO : Magari...
JOE : That's the stuff.
Now, look, I've got a sure thing.
Double your money back in two days.
GIO : Double my money?
JOE : Yeah, well, I need a little investment capital to swing the deal.
Now, if you'll just lend me a little cash, I...
GIO : Ma che son scemo?
JOE : Uh...
GIO : You owing me two months' rent -
JOE : I know, I know, I know.
GIO : And you want me to lend you money?
JOE : Yeah.
GIO : No. Certamente, no! Uh!
JOE : Tomorrow, you'll be sorry!

このイタリア語がわかればもっと楽しめる！
● Basta! は Enough! (もう十分、やめろ)。Via! は Away! (あっちへ行け)。Ciao, ragazzi. は Hi, boys. (やあ、みんな)。Magari. は I wish I could. (そうだったらいいのに)。Certamente は Certainly (確実に)。

このセリフの発音に注意！
● nobody has come, nobody has go はイタリア人の大家が話しているので [h] が発音できず nobody is come, nobody is go のように聞こえる。なお、has go は has gone の誤り。

ジョバ　：そりゃあ
ジョー　：確実な
　　　　　儲け話があって
　　　　　2日で金が2倍になる
ジョバ　：金が2倍に？
ジョー　：それには資本が要るんだが
　　　　　少し貸してくれないか

(ジョバ：バカじゃないぞ)
(ジョー：その…)
ジョバ　：2ヵ月も家賃をためてるのに
(ジョー：そうだけど)
ジョバ　：まだ貸せってか？
(ジョー：そう)
ジョバ　：ヤダね　きっぱり断る
ジョー　：明日 後悔するぞ

このニュアンスを味わう!
● **That's the stuff.** は「まさにそれだ」「それでいいんだ」という意味。**That's it.** も同じ意味で使える。**That's the spirit!** と言えば「その意気だ!」。

このセリフ、会話にいただき!
● **Tomorrow, you'll be sorry!**（明日になれば後悔するぞ）は相手のことを非難するのに使える。**Believe me, or you'll be sorry.**（僕を信じなければ後悔するぞ）のように。

Scene 16 ジョーのアパート・室内
「ジョーとアン王女の自己紹介」

So I've spent the night here...with you.
「では、ここで一晩過ごしたのね…あなたと」

JOE : Your Highness?
　　　Your Royal Highness?
ANN : Yes... what is it?
　　　Dear Dr. Bonnachoven...
JOE : Hmm? Oh, oh, sure – yes.
　　　Well, er...er, you're fine... much better.
　　　Is there anything you want?
ANN : Hmm? So many things.
JOE : Yes? Well, tell the doctor.
ANN : So... many...
JOE : Tell the good doctor everything.
ANN : Mmmmm, I dreamt and I dreamt...
JOE : Yes? Well, er, what did you dream?
ANN : I dreamt I was asleep in a street...and a young man came and he was tall and strong...and he was so mean to me.
JOE : He was?
ANN : Mmmm. It was wonderful.

...but er, from a certain angle – yes.

「でも、見方によっては
そうだな」

ジョー　　：王女様
　　　　　　王女様
アン　　　：ええ 何の用です？
　　　　　　バンノックホーベン先生
ジョー　　：（え？　そうそう）
　　　　　　かなり回復なさいました
　　　　　　何かご入り用で？
アン　　　：山ほどあるわ
（ジョー　：じゃ先生に）
アン　　　：山ほど…
ジョー　　：すべて私にお申しつけを
アン　　　：夢ばかり見ていました
ジョー　　：さようで　どんな夢をごらんに？
アン　　　：道で眠ってしまったら若い男の方がいらしたの
　　　　　　背が高くて たくましい人
　　　　　　でもとても意地悪で
ジョー　　：その人が？
アン　　　：でも素晴らしかった

JOE : Good morning.
ANN : Where's Dr. Bonnachoven?
JOE : Er, I'm afraid I don't know anybody by that name.
ANN : Wasn't I talking to him just now?
JOE : Afraid not.
ANN : Have... have I had an accident?
JOE : No.
ANN : Quite safe for me to sit up, huh?
JOE : Yeah, perfect.
ANN : Thank you.
Are these yours?
JOE : Er, did... did you lose something?
ANN : No...no.
W-would you be so kind as tell me w-where I am?
JOE : Well, this is what is laughingly known as my apartment.
ANN : Did you bring me here by force?
JOE : No, no, no, quite the contrary.
ANN : Have I been here all night...alone?
JOE : If you don't count me, yes.
ANN : So I've spent the night here...with you.
JOE : Oh, well, now, I – I don't know if I'd use those words exactly, but er, from a certain angle – yes.
ANN : How do you do?
JOE : How do you do?
ANN : And you are...?
JOE : Bradley, Joe Bradley.
ANN : Oh, uh, delighted.
JOE : You don't know how delighted I am to meet you.

ジョー	：おはよう
アン	：バンノックホーベン先生は？
ジョー	：残念ながら知らない
アン	：今 私が話してたのに
ジョー	：気のせいさ
アン	：私 事故にでも？
ジョー	：いいや
アン	：起きても大丈夫？
ジョー	：もちろん
アン	：ありがとう あなたの？
ジョー	：何か無くした？
アン	：いいえ ここがどこなのか 教えてくださる？
ジョー	：いちおう僕のアパート
アン	：無理やり私をここに？
ジョー	：むしろ その逆ですよ
アン	：ここで一夜を過ごした…私ひとりで？
ジョー	：僕を除けばね
アン	：あなたと一夜を共にしたのね？
ジョー	：その表現はあまり正確とは言えない でも、見方によってはそうだな
アン	：はじめまして
ジョー	：はじめまして
アン	：あなたは…？
ジョー	：ジョー・ブラッドレー
アン	：嬉しく思います
ジョー	：僕のほうこそ

What's your name?
「君の名前は？」

ANN : You may sit down.
JOE : Well, thank you very much.
What's your name?
ANN : Er...you may call me...Anya.
JOE : Thank you, Anya.
Would you like a cup of coffee?
ANN : What time is it?
JOE : Oh, about one thirty.
ANN : One thirty! I must get dressed and go!
JOE : Why? What's your hurry?
There's lots of time.
ANN : Oh no, there isn't and I've...I've been quite enough trouble to you as it is.
JOE : Trouble?
You're not what I'd call trouble.
ANN : I'm not?
JOE : I'll run a bath for you.
There you are.

Er...you may call me...Anya.

「あの…アーニャと
呼んでください」

アン　　：掛けてよろしい
ジョー　：これは どうも
　　　　　　君の名前は？
アン　　：私の名前は… アーニャ
ジョー　：ありがとう
　　　　　　アーニャ　コーヒーは？
アン　　：今 何時？
ジョー　：1時半ぐらい
アン　　：1時半？　すぐに行かなきゃ
ジョー　：何も急ぐことはあるまい
　　　　　　時間はある
アン　　：ないわ　これ以上
　　　　　　迷惑をおかけしては
ジョー　：迷惑だって？
　　　　　　とんでもない
アン　　：本当に？
ジョー　：お風呂の準備を
　　　　　　さあ どうぞ

What's your hurry? There's lots of time.

「何で急いでるの？
　時間はたっぷりある」

このセリフの発音に注意！
- I dreamt I was asleep in a street...and a young man came and he was tall and strong...and he was so mean to me. はかなり聞きづらい。and a や he was などがささやく感じではっきり発音されていないため。

このニュアンスを味わう！
- It was wonderful.（素晴らしかった）はジョーが意地悪だったと言いながらもアンが好意を抱いている感じ。
- Would you be so kind as to tell me where I am? は非常にていねいな言葉遣い。Would you は「もしよろしければ」という仮定の表現で控えめなニュアンス。
- I don't know if I'd use those words exactly, but er, from a certain angle - yes.「あなたと一晩過ごしたのね」とアンが表現したのに対してジョーは「そういう言葉はこの場合には適当かどうかわからない」とやんわりと否定している。from a certain angle は「ある角度からみれば」で日本語とまったく同じニュアンス。

You're not what I'd call trouble.
「迷惑なんかじゃないよ」

I'm not?
「本当に？」

このセリフ、会話にいただき！
- **What's your hurry?**（どうして急ぐの？）は反語で「そんなに急がなくてもいいのに」といった感じで使える。**There's lots of time.**（時間はたっぷりある）などと理由をつけて。
- **There you are.**（さあどうぞ、はいどうぞ）は、人に何かあげたり薦めたりするときの表現。**There you go.** や **Here you go.** も同じ意味で使えるが、カジュアルになる。

Scene 17 彫刻家のスタジオ
「相棒のカメラマンへの電話」

It's a big story. It's gotta have pictures!
「かなりの特ダネだ。写真が要るんだよ！」

JOE : Posso telefonare?
SCL : Prego, prego.
JOE : Solo un momento. Grazie.

IRV : Here we go now.
　　　There you are.
　　　That does it. Oh.
　　　Give me a little slack, will you? Pronto?
JOE : Irving! Why don't you answer the phone?
　　　Look, this is Joe.
　　　Irving, can you get over here in about five minutes?
IRV : Oh, no, I can't come now, Joe.
　　　I'm busy. Oh, no.
　　　Joe, I'm up to my ears in work.
　　　Go on, get into your next outfit, will you, honey?
　　　The canoe.
　　　What kind of a scoop, Joe?
JOE : Look, Irving, I can't talk over the telephone.

Oh, no, I can't come now, Joe. I'm busy.

「ダメだ、行けないよ
 今忙しいんだ」

ジョー ：電話を貸してくれ
彫刻家 ：どうぞ
ジョー ：すぐ済む

アビン ：さあ撮るぞ
　　　　そうだ
　　　　よし いいだろう
　　　　ちょっと休ませてくれ
ジョー ：アービング
　　　　すぐ出ろよ
　　　　5分くらいで来れるか？

アビン ：無理だ
　　　　取り込み中だよ
　　　　仕事で大変なんだ
　　　　次の衣装に着替えて
　　　　どんなネタ？

ジョー ：電話では言えない

JOE : One word in the wrong quarter and this whole thing might blow sky-high.
It's front-page stuff, that's all I can tell you.
It might be political or it might be a sensational scandal, I'm not sure which, but it's a big story.
It's got to have pictures!
IRV : But I can't come now, Joe.
I'm busy.
I'm busy now and I'm meeting Francesca at Rocca's in a half an hour and...

このセリフ、会話にいただき！
- Give me a little slack, will you?（ちょっと休ませてくれ）の Give me..., will you? は家族や親しい人に気楽に頼む表現。Give me a hand, will you?（手伝ってくれよ）、Give me some time, will you?（少し時間ちょうだい）などと使える。
- I can't talk over the telephone.（電話では話せないんだ）は、今は over the phone と略される。電話がかかってきて I can't talk right now.（今は話せないんだ）も使える。

ジョー　：話が漏れたらヤバい
　　　　　1面トップの超特ダネだ
　　　　　政治問題か 醜聞か
　　　　　とにかく大きな記事になる
　　　　　写真を

アビン　：忙しいから行けない
　　　　　それにカフェで
　　　　　彼女とデートだ

このイタリア語がわかればもっと楽しめる！
● **Posso telefonare?** は直訳では **I can telephone?**（電話使っていい?）で、**Prego** は **Please**（どうぞ）。

Scene 18 ジョーのアパート・室内
「掃除婦のアン王女への説教」

Fuori subito.
「すぐ出ていきな」

LUI : Ah! Ma guarda – cosa fa qui?
ANN : Scusi.
LUI : Ma che "scusi"? Un bel niente "scusi".
　　　Fuori subito.
ANN : Nh, nh, nh, no.
LUI : Fuori subito! Bella vita, eh? Comoda, eh?
　　　Ma lo sa, bella vita! Ma se io fossi la sua
　　　Mamma, ma sa quanti schiaffi le darei? Sciaffi
　　　da farle la faccia così! Mhhh – capito?
ANN : Nnnn...non capito. Don't understand.
LUI : Don't understand? Uhhhh! Vergogna! Eeh!

このイタリア語がわかればもっと楽しめる！
● Ma guarda. は「おや見てごらん」のことで、英語の Oh, look.
Cosa fa qui? は直訳では What you do here? で正しくは
What're you doing here?（ここで何してんの？）。Scusi は
Excuse me.

Don't understand.
「わかりません」

(ルイザ：おやまあ　ここで何を？)
(アン　：失礼)
(ルイザ：失礼もないものだ　すぐ出ていきな)
(アン　：いえ)
(ルイザ：早く！
　　　　お気楽だね
　　　　楽しい人生だね
　　　　私が母親なら顔をひっぱたくよ
　　　　分かったかい？)
アン　　：分かりません
ルイザ　："ワカリマセン？"（この恥さらし）

このイタリア語がわかればもっと楽しめる！
- **Fuori subito.** は「すぐ出ていきな」で、英語の直訳では Out soon. 正しくは Get out of here now. Bella vita は Good life（いい生活）。
- アン王女はイタリア語がわかるが、ここでは非常に早口でどなられたため動転して non capito（Don't understand.）と言っている。

Scene 19

ジョーのアパート・テラス
「ジョーとアン王女のお別れ」

There you are!
「ここにいたのか！」

JOE : There you are!
ANN : I was looking at all the people out here.
　　　　It must be fun to live in a place like this.
JOE : Yeah, it has its moments.
　　　　I can give you a running commentary on each apartment.
ANN : I must go.
JOE : Hmm?
ANN : I only waited to say goodbye.
JOE : Goodbye?
　　　　But, we've only just met.
　　　　How about some breakfast?
ANN : I'm sorry I haven't time.
JOE : Must be a pretty important date, to run off without eating.
ANN : It is.
JOE : Well, I'll go along with you, wherever you are going.

I only waited to say goodbye.
「お別れを申し上げようと
お待ちしておりました」

ジョー ：ここか
アン　 ：人通りを見ていたの

ジョー ：ここの暮らしは楽しそうね
　　　　：いろんな人が住んでる
　　　　　それぞれ紹介しよう

アン　 ：もう行きます
(ジョー：え？)
アン　 ：お別れだけ言おうと
ジョー ：お別れ？　会ったばかりじゃないか
　　　　　朝食はどう？
アン　 ：時間がないの
ジョー ：そんなに慌ててよっぽど大切な約束か

アン　 ：そうよ
ジョー ：途中までお供しよう

But, we've only just met. How about some breakfast?

「でも会ったばかりだ 朝食でもどう？」

ANN : That's all right, thank you.
　　　 I can find the place.

このセリフ、会話にいただき！
● **There you are!** は、ここでは「そこにいたんだ！」という意味。「さあどうぞ」や「はいどうぞ」と人に何かあげたり薦めたりするときにも使える。ジョーは85ページで「お風呂にどうぞ」という意味で使っている。

I'm sorry I haven't time.

「ごめんなさい
　時間がないの」

アン　　：大丈夫
　　　　　ひとりで帰れるわ

このセリフ、会話にいただき！
- **It must be fun to live in a place like this.**（こんな所に住むのは楽しいことでしょうね）の **It must be...** は「きっと…だ」と確信があるときに使う。このあとジョーも **Must be a pretty important date...**（よっぽど大事な約束なんだね）と使っている。

Scene 20 ジョーのアパート・室内
「さようなら」

Thank you for letting me sleep in your bed
「ベッドを貸してくださってありがとう」

ANN : Thank you for letting me sleep in your bed.
JOE : Oh, that's all right.
　　　Think nothing of it.
ANN : It was very considerate of you.
　　　You must have been awfully uncomfortable on that couch.
JOE : No, do it all the time!
ANN : Hm.
ANN : Goodbye, Mr. Bradley.
JOE : Goodbye.

このセリフ、会話にいただき!
● Think nothing of it. (気にしないで) は「どういたしまして」の意味もある。他に No problem. や My pleasure. なども使える。

Goodbye, Mr. Bradley.
「さようならブラッドレーさん」

Goodbye.
「さようなら」

ジョー　：ベッドを貸してくださってありがとう
ジョー　：いいんだ
　　　　　気にしないでくれ
アン　　：優しい方ね
　　　　　長椅子の寝心地は悪かったでしょう

ジョー　：いや いつものことだ
(アン　　：そう)
アン　　：さよなら ブラッドレーさん
ジョー　：さよなら

このセリフ、会話にいただき！
- It was very considerate of you.（とても思いやりのある方ね）は、うしろに to do so などが省略。ふつうは That's very considerate of you. や That's very kind of you.（ご親切ね）などと使う。

Scene 21 ジョーのアパート・中庭
「アン王女の借金」

Well...small world!
「やあ…世の中は狭いね！」

Yes.
I almost forgot
「はい。忘れるところでした」

JOE : Oh. Go right through there, and down all those steps.
ANN : Thank you.

JOE : Well...small world!
ANN : Yes – I – I almost forgot.
　　　Can you lend me some money?
JOE : Oh, yeah...that's right, you didn't have any last night did you?
ANN : Mmm.
JOE : Uh, how much...how much was it that you wanted?
ANN : Well, I don't know how much I need.
　　　How much have you got?
JOE : Well, er, suppose we just split this fifty-fifty. Here's a thousand lira.
ANN : A thousand?! Can you really spare all that?
JOE : It's about a dollar and a half.

Well, I don't know how much I need. How much have you got?

「いくら要るか分からないわ いくらお持ちなの？」

ジョー ：ここを下りればいい

アン ：ありがとう

ジョー ：世間は狭いもんだね
アン ：忘れてました
　　　　お金を貸してくださる？
ジョー ：いいとも
　　　　確か一文無しだったね
(アン ：ええ)
ジョー ：いくら必要だい？

アン ：さあ
　　　　いくらお持ちなの？
ジョー ：では半分ずつしよう
　　　　1000リラある
アン ：1000リラ　そんなにたくさん？
ジョー ：およそ1ドル50さ

ANN : Oh...well, I – I'll arrange for it to be sent back to you.
What is your address?
JOE : Er, Via Margutta 51.
ANN : Via Margutta 51. Joe Bradley.
JOE : Yeah.
ANN : Goodbye, thank you.

GIO : Ah, double my money, eh? You tell me why I double my money...that way?
JOE : Tomorrow, tomorrow, tomorrow.
GIO : Eh, tomorrow.

このセリフ、会話にいただき！
- Small world! は「世の中は狭いね！」で一番簡単な表現。It's a small world! や Small world, isn't it? や What a small world! のようなバリエーションも使える。
- I almost forgot.（忘れるところでした）はよく使われる表現。almost は「もう少しで」という意味で、I almost missed my train.（電車に乗り遅れるところだった）などと使う。

アン　　　：必ずお返しします

　　　　　　ここの住所は？
ジョー　　：マルグッタ通り51
アン　　　：マルグッタ通り51ね　　J・ブラッドリーさん
(ジョー　：そう)
アン　　　：ありがとう

ジョバ　　：金が２倍になる？
　　　　　　どうやって？
ジョー　　：明日にはな
ジョバ　　：ああ 明日ね

このニュアンスを味わう！
● **Can you lend me some money?**（お金をいくらか貸してちょうだい）で、アンは「いくらか」貸して欲しいので **some** を使っている。疑問文で **some** を使うのはまったく問題ない。「いくらでもいいから」なら **any** を使う。当時の1000リラは現在の17ドル。

このセリフ、会話にいただき！
● **I'll arrange for it to be sent back to you.**（あなたに送り返すように手配します）の後半は **to be passed on to Joe.**（ジョーに回すように）や **to be posted on the blog.**（ブログに載せるように）のように使える。

Scene 22 横町・市場
「アン王女の青空市場めぐり」

Proprio perfette, avevo raginone io, eh?
「ぴったりです、言ったとおりでしょ？」

ANN : Ah!
FRT : Lo vuole un cocomero, signore?
　　　Molto saporito.
SHO : Le vuole provare? Si?
　　　Venga, s'accomodi.
FRT : Patti chiari, lo prenda pure, molto buono, a trecento lire sole
SHO : Ha visito como le stanno bene? Proprio perfette, avevo raginone io, eh?
JOE : No...
FRT : Trecento lire sole.
JOE : No. Va be'.
FRT : Grazie.

このイタリア語がわかればもっと楽しめる！
● Molto saporito は Very tasty（とても美味しい）、Molto buono は Very good（とてもいい）という意味。molto は英語の very much のこと。

No.
「要らない」
Va be'.
「まあいいか」

(アン　　：まあ！)
(果物屋：スイカはいかが？
　　　　　とってもおいしいよ)
(靴屋　：履いてごらん
　　　　　さあ こちらに)
(果物屋：持ってみて
　　　　　おいしくてたった300)
(靴屋　：とってもよくお似合い
　　　　　言ったとおりピッタリ)

(果物屋：300リラ)
(ジョー：どうも)

このイタリア語がわかればもっと楽しめる！
- Trecento lire sole は three hundred lire only（たったの300リラ）という意味。
- Va be' は Va bene の略。英語の直訳では (It) Goes well で、ここでは Good や Okay の意味。

Scene 23　理髪店
「アン王女の大胆ショートカット」

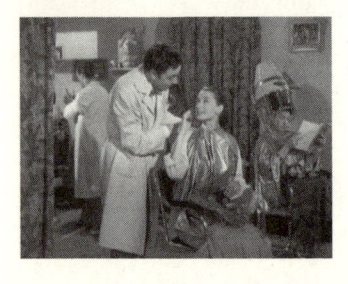

Just cut, thank you.
「カットだけしてください」

MAR :　What wonderful er, hair you have!
　　　　Messa in piega?
ANN :　Just cut, thank you.
MAR :　Just cut?
　　　　Well — then, cut, er, so?
ANN :　Higher.
MAR :　Higher?
　　　　Here?
ANN :　More.
MAR :　Here?
ANN :　Even more.
MAR :　Where?
ANN :　There.
MAR :　There.
　　　　Are you sure, Miss?
ANN :　I'm quite sure, thank you.
MAR :　All off?
ANN :　All off.
MAR :　Off! Are you sure?

Just cut?
Well – then,
cut, er, so?

「カットだけ?
では、このくらい?」

マリオ　：美しい髪をお持ちですね
　　　　　ウェーブは?
アン　　：カットだけで
マリオ　：カットだけ?
　　　　　では これぐらいですか?
アン　　：もっと上で
マリオ　：もっと上?
　　　　　これぐらい?
アン　　：もっと
マリオ　：ここ?
アン　　：もっとよ
マリオ　：どの辺り?
アン　　：ここよ
マリオ　：そこか
　　　　　本気かい?
アン　　：いたって本気よ
マリオ　：これ全部?
アン　　：これ全部
マリオ　：カット　本当にいいの?

More.
「もっと上」
Here?
「ここ？」
Even more.
「さらに上」

ANN : Yes!
MAR : Yes. Off! off! off!

このイタリア語がわかればもっと楽しめる！
- **Messa in piega?** は英語の直訳では Put a (permanent) wave? で、「ウエーブをかける？」と理髪師はたずねている。

Are you sure, Miss?
「本当にいいんですね、お嬢さん?」

I'm quite sure, thank you.
「本当にいいわ、ありがとう」

(アン　：はい)
マリオ　：それではカット　カット　カット！

このセリフ、会話にいただき！
- **Are you sure, Miss?** と理髪師がアンにたずねているが、これは相手の意向を確認するのによく使われる。**Are you sure you don't want a drink?**（本当にお酒要らないの？）のように。答え方はアンの **I'm quite sure.** の他に **Positive.** など。

Scene 24 バー・電話
「電話使用中」

Ragazzi!
「君たち！」

MAN : Vostra moglie...non c'entra affatto!
　　　Assolutamente...e che...!
JOE : Ragazzi!
MAN : Oh no, no, no, no...!

理髪店
「ヘアカット中」

MAR : Off! Ah.

このイタリア語がわかればもっと楽しめる！
● **Vostra moglie...non c'entra affatto!** は「あんたの奥さんとはまったく関係のないことだ」という意味。**Vostra moglie** は Your wife で、**non c'entra affatto** は英語の直訳では Your wife is not in at all. となる。

Off! Ah.
「カット！ ふう」

(男性　：あんたの奥さんとは関係ないことだ
　　　　　絶対に　とんでもない)
(ジョー：君たち！)
(男性　：いや違う違う…！)

マリオ　：カット！　ふう

このイタリア語がわかればもっと楽しめる！
- Assolutamente...e che...! は「絶対に…とんでもない！」という意味。Assolutamente は Absolutely のこと。che はここでは驚きを表す。
- Ragazzi! は「子どもたち！」という呼びかけ。Boys and girls!ということ。ragazzo が boy で ragazza が girl。入り交じった複数形が ragazzi。

Scene 25 トレビの泉
「ジョーのカメラ探し」

Er, you don't mind if I just borrow it, do you?
「あの、ちょっと借りてもいいよね？」

JOE : That's a nice-looking camera you have there.
Ah, it's nice. Mmmm.
Er, you don't mind if I just borrow it, do you?
GAL : Miss Weber!
JOE : I'll give it back. Just for a couple of minutes.
GAL : No! Go, it's my camera.

このセリフの発音に注意！
● 脚本を読むと That's a nice-looking camera you have there. となっているが、ジョーは nice-looking を nice-little のように発音している。

I'll give it back.
「返すから」

ジョー　：いいカメラを持ってるね

　　　　　おじさんに貸してくれる？
女の子　：ウェバー先生
ジョー　：2・3分だけ
女の子　：イヤ　放して　私のカメラよ

このトリビアで通になろう！
● 「トレビの泉」の由来は伝説でTriviaという名の乙女が兵士たちに泉のありかを教えたため。Trivia は Tri（3つ）の via（道）のこと。泉の前から3本の道がのびているからという説ともあわさっている。**Trivia**（トリビア）が「ささいなこと、雑学的知識」になったのは中世の大学の教養3科目（文法、弁証、修辞学）が他の教養4科目（天文学、幾何学、算術、音楽）よりも劣るという皮肉から。

Scene 26 理髪店
「カット終了とダンスへの誘い」

It's just what I wanted.
「まさにこうしたかったの」

MAR : You musician, maybe?
　　　You artist? Aha? Painter...?
　　　I know, you modella! Model, huh?
ANN : Thank you.
MAR : Ecco qua finito! It's perfect!
ANN : Oh.
MAR : Y-y-you be nice without long hair.
　　　Now, it's cool, hmm? Cool?
ANN : Yes, it's, it's just what I wanted.
MAR : Grazie. Now, why you not come dancing tonight with me?
　　　You should see — it's so nice — it's on a boat on the Tevere, Tiber — the river by Sant' Angelo.
　　　Moonlight, music, romantico!
　　　Is very, very...very!
　　　Please, you come?
ANN : I wish I could.
MAR : Oh. But, but, your friend I not think they recog... nize you.

Now, why you not come dancing tonight with me?

「今晩一緒に踊りに行かない?」

マリオ　：あなたは音楽家かな?
　　　　　芸術家?　画家?
　　　　　分かった　モデルだ　モデルだな?
アン　　：お上手ね
マリオ　：できました　完ぺきです
(アン　　：あら)
マリオ　：短いほうがお似合いです
　　　　　とても素敵ですよ
アン　　：こうしたかったの
マリオ　：今夜　僕と一緒に踊りに行きませんか

　　　　　いい所ですよ
　　　　　お城のそばテヴェレ川の船の上です
　　　　　月明かりの下の音楽ロマンチックです

　　　　　来てください
アン　　：残念ですけど
マリオ　：きっと友達は誰も
　　　　　あなたと気づきませんよ

ANN : No, I don't think they will!
MAR : Oh, thank you very much.
ANN : Thank you.
MAR : Ah, er, signorina.
After nine o'clock, I'll be there.
Dancing on river. Remember Sant'Angelo.
All my friends...if you come, you will be most pretty of all girl!
ANN : Thank you. Goodbye.
MAR : Goodbye.

このイタリア語がわかればもっと楽しめる!
- modella は「女性のモデル」のことで、「男性モデル」は modello。英語ではどちらも model。
- Ecco qua finito! は「さあこれで終わった!」という意味。英語の直訳は Here now finished!

このセリフの発音に注意!
- 理髪師は You be nice without long hair. (長い髪でなくても素敵だ) と言っているが、脚本を読むと You look nice without long hair. となっている。イタリア人なので間違っているが意味は通じる。

アン	：そうね 気づかないわね
(マリオ	：これはどうも)
アン	：ありがとう
マリオ	：（あの、お嬢さん）
	9時に待っています
	サンタンジェロです
	来てくれたら
	あなたが一番の美人です
アン	：ご親切に
マリオ	：さよなら

このセリフ、会話にいただき！
● **I wish I could.**（そうできたらいいのですが）は、誘いをことわるときに使えるほか、本当にそう望んでいるときにも使える。**I wish I could come to the party.**（パーティに行けたらいいのですが）など。
このイタリア語がわかればもっと楽しめる！
● **signorina** は「お嬢さま」で、未婚女性への敬称。

Scene 27 スペイン広場
「アン王女とアイスクリームと花」

Er, gelato?
「あの、アイスクリームを？」
Gelato.
「アイスクリーム」
Thank you.
「ありがとう」

ICE : Aranciate? Gazzose? Chinotto? Gelato?
ANN : Er, gelato?
ICE : Gelato.
ANN : Thank you.
ICE : Grazie. Signorina...il resto.
ANN : Oh, grazie.
PRT : Mi dia un gelato di cioccolata e crema, per favore.
FLR : Ooooohh, brava signorina, guardi, qui ci sono dei fiori per lei.
　　　Garofani, sono vennuti da Bordighera, freschi, guardi, che bellezza! Grazie.
ANN : Thank you.
FLR : Mille lire. Ein Tausend Lire.
ANN : Oh...no money.
FLR : No?
ANN : No.
FLR : Ottocento lire, va bene?
ANN : I...I'm sorry, I have really no money.

I'm sorry, I've really no money.

「ごめんなさい、本当にお金が
 ありません」

(菓子屋 : ジュース レモネードに
　　　　　アイスクリームはいかが？)
(アン　 : アイスクリームを)
(菓子屋 : アイスクリームね)
アン　　: ありがとう
(菓子屋 : お嬢さん お釣り)
(アン　 : ありがとう)
(聖職者 : チョコレートとクリーム味を1つ)
(花屋　 : お嬢さんに
　　　　　お似合いの花ですよ
　　　　　摘みたてできれいでしょう)

(アン　 : ありがとう)
(花屋　 : 1000リラです)
アン　　: お金ないわ
花屋　　: ない？
(アン　 : はい)
(花屋　 : 800リラでどう？)
アン　　: 本当にお金ないの

FLR : E troppo pure questo? Settecento di piu non eh, non posso fare.
ANN : Look. I'm sorry.
FLR : Ecco, prego. Ah, buona fortuna!
ANN : Grazie!
FLR : Niente.
ANN : Grazie

このイタリア語がわかればもっと楽しめる！
- Gelato はイタリアの ice cream のこと、日本語でも「ジェラート」と呼ぶ。
- il resto は「お釣り」で、英語の the change のこと。Tenga il resto. と言えば Keep the change.（お釣りはとっといて）という意味。
- Va bene? は直訳では Goes well? で、ここでは Okay? や All right? の意味。

(花屋　：じゃ700だ
　　　　　これ以上はムリ)
アン　　：見て　ごめんなさい
(花屋　：どうぞ　幸運を！)
(アン　：ありがとう)
(花屋　：いいえ)
(アン　：ありがとう)

このイタリア語がわかればもっと楽しめる！
- Mille lire は「1000リラ」で、mille は thousand のこと。Ein Tausend Lire はドイツ語で A thousand lire のこと。
- Ottocento lire, va bene? は「800リラでどう？」と値下げをしている。Otto は Eight、cento は hundred のこと。
- Grazie! は Thank you! で Niente は直訳では Nothing. Not at all.（どういたしまして）といった意味。

Scene 28 スペイン広場の階段
「アン王女の告白と休日の始まり」

Weeell, it's you!
「なんと、君か！」
Yes, Mr. Bradley!
「そうよ私よ！」
Or is it?
「違う人かな？」

JOE : Weeell, it's you!
ANN : Yes, Mr. Bradley!
JOE : Or is it?
ANN : Do you like it?
JOE : Yeah...very much.
So that was your mysterious appointment.
ANN : Mr. Bradley, I have a confession to make.
JOE : Confession?
ANN : Yes, I...ran away last night – from school.
JOE : Oh, what was the matter?
Trouble with the teacher?
ANN : No, nothing like that.
JOE : Well, you don't just run away from school for nothing.
ANN : Well, I only meant it to be for an hour or two.
They gave me something last night to make me sleep.
JOE : Oh, I see.
ANN : Now I'd better get a taxi and go back.

I have a confession to make.
「告白することがあるの」
Confession?
「告白?」

ジョー　：おや 君だったのか
アン　　：そうよ私よ
ジョー　：違う人かな?
アン　　：似合ってる?
ジョー　：とっても
　　　　　これが例の約束だったのか
アン　　：告白することがあるの
ジョー　：告白?
アン　　：昨晩 逃げ出してきたの　学校から
ジョー　：どうしたの?
　　　　　先生とトラブルでも
アン　　：全然 違うわ
ジョー　：何か理由でも?

アン　　：1・2時間のつもりだったの
　　　　　でも睡眠薬を打たれたから

ジョー　：なるほど
アン　　：もうタクシーに乗って帰らなければ

But don't you have to work?
「でもお仕事は？」
Work? No!
「仕事？ ないよ！」

JOE : Well, look, before you do, why don't you take a little time for yourself?
ANN : Maybe another hour.
JOE : Live dangerously, take the whole day!
ANN : I could do some of the things I've always wanted to.
JOE : Like what?
ANN : Oh, you can't imagine... I'd, I'd like to do just whatever I'd like, the whole day long!
JOE : You mean, things like having your hair cut? Eating gelato?
ANN : Yes, and I'd, I'd like to sit at a sidewalk cafe and look in shop windows, walk in the rain!
Have fun, and maybe some excitement.
It doesn't seem much to you, does it?
JOE : It's great! Tell you what.
Why don't we do all those things – together?
ANN : But don't you have to work?

Today's gonna be a holiday.
「今日は、休みにするよ」

ジョー　：待てよ　その前に
　　　　　もう少しゆっくりしたら
アン　　：1時間くらいなら
ジョー　：思いきってまる一日にしたら
アン　　：したいことができるわ

ジョー　：例えば?
アン　　：あなたには想像もつかない
　　　　　いろんなことよ
ジョー　：例えば散髪や食べ歩き?

アン　　：そう　カフェのテラス席に座るわ
　　　　　ショーウィンドーを眺め雨の中を歩くの
　　　　　楽しくて　ワクワクすること
　　　　　あなたにはありふれてるわね
ジョー　：素晴らしいさ
　　　　　そんなの全部やろうよ　2人で一緒に
アン　　：お仕事は?

JOE : Work? No!
　　　Today's going to be a holiday.
ANN : But you don't want to do a lot of silly things.
JOE : Don't I? First wish – one sidewalk cafe –
　　　coming right up! – I know just the place –
　　　Rocca's.

このニュアンスを味わう!

- Well, it's you!（おや、君か！）と言ったあとの Or is it? は、Or is it really you?（本当に君なのか？）の略。ジョーがアンのイメージチェンジを認めたうえで遊び心を表現したもの。アンが嬉しそうに Do you like it? と返事する。
- Well, you don't just run away from school for nothing. でジョーは一般論にして、「人は訳もなく学校から逃げ出したりはしないよ」と直接アンを責めるのを避けている。people より you のほうが、温かい感じの言い方になる。なお、アンのことを直接言うなら Well, you didn't just run away... と過去形にするはず。

ジョー　：今日は休みにする

アン　　：遊びに付き合うの？
ジョー　：まずはカフェのテラス席からだ
　　　　　いい場所を知ってる

このセリフ、会話にいただき！
● Tell you what.（話を聞いて、こうしよう）は I('ll) tell you what. の略でカジュアルな言い方。人に何か提案するときに使う。Tell you what. Why don't we go to a movie?（こうしよう、映画に行こうよ）。

このトリビアで通になろう！
● カフェの名前 G.Rocca は有名な Cafe Greco（カフェ・グレコ）のもじり。Greco は Greek（ギリシャの）。実際にはそこで撮影されていない。La Piazza di Spagna は「スペイン広場」で、英語では The Spanish Square。「スペイン階段」は The Spanish Steps と言う。

Scene 29 ロッカズ・カフェ
「お互いの詮索と相棒カメラマン」

> Hey, er, anybody tell you you're a dead ringer for...
>
> 「あの、君は誰かに"クリソツ"って…」

JOE : What will the people at school say when they see your new haircut?
ANN : They'll have a fit.
What would they say if they knew I'd spent the night in your room?
JOE : Well, er, I'll tell you what, you don't tell your folks and I won't tell mine.
ANN : It's a pact.
JOE : Now, what would you like to drink?
ANN : Champagne, please.
JOE : Er, commerierie, er...
WAT : Comandi, signore.
JOE : Champagne?
WAT : Si, si.
JOE : Well, er, champagne per la senorina and er, cold coffee for me.
WAT : Va bene, signore.
JOE : Must be quite a life you have in that school – champagne for lunch.

It's an American term and er, and it means er, anyone who has a great deal of charm.

「それはアメリカの表現で、えー、
　すごく魅力的な人のことさ」

ジョー　　：学校の人たちが
　　　　　　その髪を見たら？
アン　　　：ひきつけを起こすでしょうね
　　　　　　泊まったことを知ったら？
　　　　　　（あなたの部屋に）
ジョー　　：誰にも言うなよ
　　　　　　僕も言わない
アン　　　：約束ね
ジョー　　：さて 何を飲む？
アン　　　：シャンパンを
（ジョー　：あの…）
（ボーイ　：ご注文は？）
ジョー　　：シャンパンある？
（ボーイ　：あります）
ジョー　　：お嬢さんにシャンパンと
　　　　　　僕にアイスコーヒー
（ボーイ　：かしこまりました）
ジョー　　：昼食にシャンパンとは
　　　　　　すごい生活だね

ANN : Only on special occasions.
JOE : For instance?
ANN : The last was my father's anniversary.
JOE : Wedding?
ANN : No, it was...the fortieth anniversary of umm...of the day he got his job.
JOE : Forty years on the job.
What do you know about that?
What does he do?
ANN : Well...mostly you might call it...public relations.
JOE : Oh, well, that's hard work.
ANN : Yes, I wouldn't care for it.
JOE : Does he?
ANN : I've...heard him complain about it.
JOE : Why doesn't he quit?
ANN : Well, people in that line of work almost never do quit — unless it's actually unhealthy for them to continue.
JOE : Uh-huh. Well, here's to his health, then.
ANN : You know, that's what everybody says.
JOE : It's all right?
ANN : Yes, thank you. What is your work?
JOE : Oh, I'm...er, in the selling game.
ANN : Really? How interesting.
JOE : Uh-huh.
ANN : What do you sell?
JOE : Er, fertilizer, er, chemicals, you know?
Chemicals — stuff like that.
ANN : Hum.
JOE : Un-huuh. Irving!
Well, am I glad to see you!

アン　　：特別な時だけ
ジョー　：どんな時？
アン　　：父の記念日だとか
ジョー　：結婚記念日？
アン　　：いいえ 父の在位…
　　　　　在職40周年の記念日よ
ジョー　：在職40周年か
　　　　　驚いたな
　　　　　仕事は何を？
アン　　：一種の広報みたいなものかしら
ジョー　：それは大変な仕事だね
アン　　：私は好きになれない
ジョー　：お父さんも？
アン　　：時々 グチをこぼしているわ
ジョー　：辞めればいい
アン　　：この仕事に関わると
　　　　　勝手には辞めれないの
　　　　　病気とかにならない限り
ジョー　：では 父上の健康を祝して
アン　　：実はみんな そう言うのよ
ジョー　：おいしい？
アン　　：ええとっても　何のお仕事を？
ジョー　：物を売る仕事さ
アン　　：面白そうね
（ジョー　：まあね）
アン　　：品物は？
ジョー　：肥料だとか 薬品だとか
　　　　　そういったもの
（アン　　：へえ）
ジョー　：アービング
　　　　　よく来たな

IRV :	Why — did you forget your wallet?
JOE :	Er, pull up a chair, Irving, sit down with us here.
IRV :	Aren't you going to introduce me?
JOE :	Er, yes, this is a very good friend of mine, Irving Radovich. Anya, Irving.
IRV :	Anya...?
ANN :	Smith.
IRV :	Oh, hiya Smitty.
ANN :	Charmed.
IRV :	Hey, er, anybody tell you you're a dead ringer for...Oh! Well...uh...I guess I'll be going.
JOE :	Oh, don't do a thing like that, Irving. Sit down, join us, join us, join us.
IRV :	Well er, just till Francesca gets here.
ANN :	Tell me, Mr. er, er, Radovich, er, what is a ringer?
IRV :	Oh, eh, waiter! Whiskey, please.
JOE :	It's an American term and er, and it means er, anyone who has a great deal of charm.
ANN :	Oh. Thank you.
IRV :	You're welcome. Er.
GAL :	Ciao, Irving.
GAL :	Ciao.
IRV :	Oh, ciao...
ANN :	Er, Mis...
IRV :	Cousins.
ANN :	M...Mr. Bradley's just been telling me all about his work.
IRV :	Mmm, I'd like to have heard that.
ANN :	What do you do?
IRV :	I'm the same racket as Joe. Only I'm a photo...
ANN :	Ah...oh!

アビン	：財布でも忘れたか
ジョー	：まあ 座れよ
アビン	：紹介してよ
ジョー	：アービング・ラドヴィッチ
	彼女はアーニャだ
アビン	：アーニャ…
アン	：スミスよ
アビン	：よろしく
アン	：光栄ですわ
アビン	：誰かに"クリソツ"って言われた…
	どうやらお邪魔らしい
ジョー	：まさか そんなことない
	いいから座れよ
アビン	：それじゃ 彼女が来るまで
アン	：ラドヴィッチさん"クリソツ"って何？
(アビン	：あの ウィスキーを)
ジョー	：アメリカ独特の言い回しで
	とても魅力的な人を指すんだ
アン	：まあ ありがとう
アビン	：どういたしまして
(女性	：こんにちは)
(女性	：こんにちは)
(アビン	：やあ)
(アン	：あの…)
アビン	：いとこだ
アン	：ブラッドレーさんの
	仕事の話を聞いてたの
アビン	：聞きたかったな
アン	：あなたは何を？
アビン	：ジョーと同じ職業だが…
(アン	：あら…まあ！)

JOE :	I'm awfully sorry, Irving!
IRV :	W-w-wha-? What are you-?
JOE :	I'm sorry, Irving.
IRV :	Look, I can take a hint!
	I'll see you around.
ANN :	Oh, your drink's just here; please sit down...
JOE :	Yes, here's your drink right now, Irving.
	Take it easy. I'm sorry about that.
	Sit down, that's a good fellow.
	Have a...that's a boy.
IRV :	You're t - You're twisting my arm, you know.
JOE :	Just – just be a little more careful not to spill...
IRV :	Spill? Who's been doing the spilling?
JOE :	You.
IRV :	Me?
JOE :	Yeah.
IRV :	Where did you find this looney?
	You're okay. Here's to you, huh?
	Here's hoping for the best.
	If it...if it wasn't for that hair, I – I – I'd swear that...
MNK :	S'e fatto male?
MNK :	Ha bisogno aiuto?
IRV :	Thanks.
ANN :	Oh! Have you hurt yourself? Oh...
JOE :	You slipped, Irving.
IRV :	Slipped?
JOE :	You slipped. You almost hurt yourself that time!
IRV :	I slipped?!
JOE :	Yes.
IRV :	I almost hurt myself?

ジョー　：これは悪いことしたな
アビン　：一体 何なんだ
ジョー　：すまない
アビン　：気を利かせるさ
　　　　　また 近いうちに
アン　　：飲み物も来たわ
ジョー　：落ち着け
　　　　　僕が悪かったよ
　　　　　さあ 座ってくれ
　　　　　君の飲み物だ
アビン　：そこまで勧めるならいてやろう
ジョー　：こぼさないように気をつけなきゃ
アビン　：こぼす？　誰のせいだ？
ジョー　：君だよ
アビン　：僕だって？
(ジョー　：そう)
アビン　：この男おかしいよ
　　　　　君はステキさ
　　　　　幸運を祈って乾杯
　　　　　この髪型さえ違ったら
　　　　　絶対に似て…
(修道士　：大丈夫？)
(修道士　：さあお手を)
アビン　：どうも
(アン　　：まあ　ケガは？)
(ジョー　：滑ったな)
(アビン　：滑った？)
ジョー　：滑ったよ ケガするところだ
アビン　：僕が滑った？
(ジョー　：そう)
(アビン　：ケガするところ？)

JOE : You did hurt yourself...behind the ear, I think. You've got a bad sprain there...
IRV : Joe, I didn't slip!
Never mind I got a bad sprain, Joe.
JOE : We'd better go in here and get it fixed up, pal. I want to talk to you.
IRV : Well, yeah, I'd like to...
JOE : Will you excuse us for a minute, Anya?
ANN : Yes, of course. I- I'm so sorry.
IRV : If I slipped, I slipped...

このニュアンスを味わう！

- You don't tell your folks and I won't tell mine. で「お互いに家族に言うのはやめよう」とジョーが言うとアンはIt's a pact.（約束よ）と言う。2人だけの秘密を持つことで親密さが増してきている。
- Well, am I glad to see you! と主語と動詞を入れ換えて、ジョーがアービングが来た嬉しさをモロに表現している。
- ringerは「そっくりさん、ウリふたつ、クリソツ」の意味で、deadは強調語で exact や perfect と同じ。a dead ringer は an exact double のこと。昔は偽造者、にせ金造りを意味した。競馬で本物によく似た馬を出場させたときに鐘を鳴らしたのが語源。アンが知らない俗語ということで〝クリソツ〟の訳が最適。
- アンは ringer が「魅力的な人」の意味と思っている。船上パーティのシーンでジョーに I think you're a ringer. と言うのはそのため。
- racket は俗語で「職業」のこと。
- Look, I can take a hint! の take a hint は、周りの状況を見て「気がきく」という意味だが、ここでは「そこまでしなくてもわかるよ！」というニュアンス。
- If I slipped, I slipped... は「すべったのなら、すべったのかな…」。ジョーはアービングにアン王女のことはしゃべるなと暗に伝えているのだがいっこうにピンとこない。

ジョー　：ケガをしてるよ
　　　　　耳のうしろがむち打ちだ
アビン　：むち打ちなんかどうでもいい

(ジョー　：中に入って手当を
　　　　　話もある)
(アビン　：ああ僕も…)
ジョー　：失礼しても？
アン　　：ええ どうぞ　お大事に

このセリフ、会話にいただき！
- **What would you like to drink?**（何をお飲みになりますか？）は とてもていねい。**(Would you) care for something to drink?** も 同じように使える。答え方もていねいにアンの **Champagne, please.** か **I'd like some Champagne.** と言うほうがいい。
- **Here's to his health.**（お父さまに乾杯）は形を変えて、**Here's to you.**（あなたに乾杯）や **Here's hopin' for the best.**（幸運を祈って）などと使える。
- ジョーの **Will you excuse us for a minute, Anya?**（ちょっと失礼してもいいかな、アーニャ？）は、日常でもよく使われる。ちょっと席を立つ場合や人払いをするときなどに **Will you excuse me?** や **Would you excuse us?** と使える。**Would** を使うとていねい。

このダブル・ミーニングでにやり！
- **spill** には「（液体などを）こぼす」と「（秘密などを）もらす」の2 つの意味があり、ジョーは2つをかけてアービングに注意している。 **slip** には「すべる」と「口をすべらす」の意味があるし、**hurt** にも「傷つく」と「困る」の意味がある。

Scene 30

ロッカズ・カフェの中
「ジョーとアービングの密約」

> ### This is my story. I dug it up, I gotta protect it!
> 「これは僕の特ダネだ。見つけ出したんだ。守らなきゃ！」

IRV : Now wait, now wait, just a minute, let...look, Joe, what are you trying to do?
Now take your hands off!
JOE : Have you got your lighter?
IRV : What's that got to do with it?
JOE : Have you got it?
IRV : Yeah, but what are you trying to do to me?
JOE : Listen, what would you do for five grand?
IRV : Five grand?
JOE : Yeah. Now, look, she doesn't know who I am or what I do.
Look, Irving, this is my story.
I dug it up, I got to protect it!
IRV : She's really the...?
JOE : Ssssh! Your tintypes are going to make this little epic twice as valuable.
IRV : "The Princess Goes Slumming."
JOE : You're in for twenty-five percent of the take.
IRV : And the take's five 'G'?

Ssh, you want in on this deal or don't you?

「シー、この話に
乗るのか乗らないのか？」

アビン　：一体 何のマネだ
　　　　　　僕から手を放せよ

ジョー　：ライター持ってるか？
アビン　：それがどうした？
(ジョー　：持ってるか？)
(アビン　：ああ　で僕に何を？)
ジョー　：5000ドルあったら何をする？
アビン　：5000ドル？
ジョー　：彼女は僕が何者か知らない
　　　　　　僕の特ダネだ
　　　　　　気づかれては困る

アビン　：彼女は本物の…
ジョー　：写真が付くと価値は倍だ

アビン　："王女の冒険"
ジョー　：君の分は25パーセント
アビン　：5000ドルのか

JOE : Minimum. Henessey shook hands on it.
IRV : ...seven, five.
That's...that's fifteen hundred dollars!
JOE : It's twelve-fifty.
IRV : Okay, now you shake.
JOE : Okay, now, lend me thirty thousand.
IRV : Thirty th-? That's fifty bucks! You going to buy the crown jewels?
JOE : She's out there now, drinking champagne that I can't pay for!
We got to entertain her, don't we?
IRV : Joe, we can't go running around town with a... hot princess!
JOE : Ssh, you want in on this deal or don't you?
IRV : This I want back Saturday.
JOE : Okay, now where's your lighter?
Let's go to work.

このセリフ、会話にいただき！
- What's that got to do with it? (それとこれと何の関係があるんだ？) はよく使われる表現。have to do with は口語では have got to do with となる。I've got nothing to do with it. (私はそれと何の関係もない) なども使える。

このニュアンスを味わう！
- "The Princess Goes Slumming." は「王女様、スラム街を行く」ということだが、「特に好奇心でスラム街を見物する」というニュアンス。five 'G' (grand) は5000ドルで、fifty bucks は50ドル。

ジョー	：支局長の保証済み
アビン	：つまり1500ドルか
ジョー	：1250ドルだよ
アビン	：契約成立だ
ジョー	：それじゃ3万リラ貸せ
アビン	：50ドルだぞ
	王冠でも買うのか
ジョー	：シャンパンを頼んだし
	（金がないんだ）
	楽しませなきゃ
アビン	：王女を連れ回せないだろ
ジョー	：やるのか？
	やらないのか？
アビン	：土曜には返せよ
ジョー	：分かった　ライターは？
	よし　仕事だ

このニュアンスを味わう!

● **You going to buy the crown jewels?** は、アービングがジョーから大金を貸せと言われて「王冠でも買ってあげるのか？」と皮肉る。**a hot princess** は「やばい王女さま」。hot は「話題の、物議をかもす」の意味。

このトリビアで通になろう!

● ジョーが **lend me thirty thousand**（3万リラ貸せ）と言うとアービングが **That's fifty bucks!**（そりゃ50ドルだぜ！）と驚く。当時の1000リラは現在の17ドルくらいで、3万リラは現在の510ドル。

● **five 'G'**（5000ドル）は現在の約5万ドルで、特ダネをものにすればジョーは37,500ドル、アービングは12,500ドルもらえることになる。

Scene 31 ロッカズ・カフェのテーブル
「アン王女の初めてのタバコ」

Nothing to it.
「簡単だわ」

That's right – nothing to it.
「そうさ、簡単さ」

ANN : Better now?
IRV : Huh?
ANN : Your ear.
IRV : My ear? Oh, yeah, er, Joe fixed it.
　　　Er, would you care for a cigarette?
ANN : Yes, please.
　　　You won't believe this – but it's my very first.
JOE : Your very first?
ANN : Mm-hm.
IRV : Oh...
JOE : No, er, smoking in school, hmm?
IRV : Your first cigarette...
　　　There, gismo works.
JOE : Well, what's the verdict, er... okay?
ANN : Nothing to it.
IRV : That's right – nothing to it.
JOE : Er, commerierie.
WAT : Comandi.
JOE : Conto, per favore.

She's a grand girl, Irving, grand.
Er, five grand, Irving.

「素敵な娘だよな、アービング、素敵で、えー、5000ドルの輝きだ」

アン　　：良くなった？
アビン　：何が？
アン　　：耳の具合
アビン　：耳？　ジョーがすっかり治してくれた
　　　　　タバコはいかが？
アン　　：ええ　頂くわ
　　　　　吸うのは これが初めてよ
ジョー　：これが初めてか
(アン　　：ええ)
(アビン　：へえ…)
ジョー　：学校では禁止なのか
アビン　：初めてのタバコ
　　　　　うまくいった
ジョー　：ご感想は？　大丈夫かい？
アン　　：簡単だわ
アビン　：そうさ 簡単さ
(ジョー　：ウェイター)
(ボーイ　：何でしょうか)
ジョー　：勘定を頼む

IRV : Stretch my legs a little, here.
ANN : Hm.
JOE : I'll pick this one up, Irving.
IRV : Yeah, you can afford it.
JOE : Well, what shall we do next?
Shall we, er, make out a little schedule?
ANN : Oh, no, not that word, please!
JOE : Va bene.
Oh, I didn't mean a work sche - school schedule- I meant, er, a fun schedule.
ANN : Yes, let's just go, huh?
JOE : Well, how about you, Irving?
Are you ready?
IRV : Er, yeah.
JOE : Let's go.
FRN : Ciao, Irving, come stai?
IRV : Francesca. Oh, er, this is...
ANN : Smitty.
JOE : She's a grand girl, Irving, grand.
Er, five grand, Irving. Ciao.
IRV : Joe!
FRN : Where are you going now?
IRV : Honey, I got to work.
I'll call you tonight.

アビン　：僕も一服するか

ジョー　：これは僕が払うよ
アビン　：金があるからな
ジョー　：次は何をする？
　　　　　日程を決めようか
アン　　：その言葉は使わないで
ジョー　：（どうも）
　　　　　学校行事の日程じゃない
　　　　　遊びのスケジュールだよ
アン　　：じゃあ 行きましょう
ジョー　：（君はどうだ？）
　　　　　用意はいいか？
（アビン：ああ）
ジョー　：行こうか
（フラン：こんにちは　元気？）
アビン　：フランチェスカ　こちらは…
アン　　：スミッティ
ジョー　：素敵な娘だよな 素敵だ
　　　　　5000ドルの輝きだ
（アビン：ジョー！）
フラン　：どこへ行くの？
アビン　：仕事だ
　　　　　今夜 電話する

They were supposed to be inconspicuous.
「目立たないように
　するはずでは」

空港
「秘密諜報部員の到着」

AMB : Look at those men! They were supposed to be inconspicuous.
GEN : You asked for plain clothes.

このセリフ、会話にいただき！
- Would you care for a cigarette?(タバコいかがでしょうか？)の Would you care for... は非常にていねいな申し出。Would you care for something to drink?(何かお飲み物はいかがでしょうか？)などと使える。

このニュアンスを味わう！
- Well, what's the verdict...(判決はどうでしょう)とジョーはタバコがまずいのではと心配して言ったのだが、アンはうまくタバコが吸えるかどうかを気にしていたために Nothing to it.(何でもないわ)と答えた。なお、Conto, per favore. は英語の Check, please.

You asked for plain clothes.

「私服をお望みでしたから」

大使　：連中を見ろ
　　　　あれで目立たないつもりか
将軍　：私服でとおっしゃったので

このニュアンスを味わう!
- **Stretch my legs** は「長く座っていたので足をほぐして一服する」というニュアンス。

このダブル・ミーニングでにやり!
- **She's a grand girl...** でジョーは grand を「素敵な」と「1000ドル」の両方にかけている。**five grand** を「5000ドルの輝きだ」とすれば両方の意味が出せる。

このセリフ、会話にいただき!
- **I'll pick this one up.**（これは僕は払うよ）の this one は the tab（勘定書き）のこと。pick up the tab で「勘定を払う」。I'll pick up the tab. と使える。

Scene 32　ヴェネツィア広場の通り
「スクーターの乱暴運転」

Hey!
「おい！」

JOE : Hey! Scusi. Hey!
　　　　Stop, come back before people get hit!
ANN : Whoa!
JOE : Hey, come back.
　　　　You can't drive this thing.

　　　　Let me take this. Let me take over.
ANN : No, no, no. I- I can do it.

**Lemme take this.
Lemme take over.**
「僕がやるよ。僕にまかせて」

ジョー　：待てよ
　　　　　　止まれ
(アン　　：わー！)
ジョー　：運転しちゃダメだ

　　　　　　僕がやるよ　僕にまかせて
アン　　　：いや　私できます

Scene 33 警察署
「ジョーたちの必死の説得」

American News Service? What did he mean?
「アメリカン・ニュース社？どういうこと？」

JOE : Ah. Uh.
IRV : Oh...I'm going straight from now on.
ANN: American News Service?
 What did he mean?
JOE : Huh? Oh, well, you know, you say you're with the press and you can get away with anything.
IRV : Yeah...ha!
 Go to church to get married on a scooter —
 that's a hot one! Joe's a wonderful liar!
MAN : Tanti bei bambini cosi. Auguri, eh. Auguri...
IRV : Ciao.
ANN: You don't have to look so worried.
 I won't hold you to it.
JOE : Thank you very much.
ANN: You don't have to be too grateful!
JOE : Okay, I won't.
ANN: I'm a good liar too, aren't I, Mr. Bradley?
JOE : The best I ever met.
IRV : Uh-huh!

I won't hold you to it.
「結婚してとは言わないわ」

(ジョー ：やれやれ)
アビン ：これから まじめにやる
アン ："アメリカン・ニュース社"って？
　　　　（どういうこと？）
ジョー ：記者だと言えば
　　　　大目に見てくれるんだ
アビン ：結婚式に向かってた？
　　　　（あれは傑作だ！）
　　　　彼はウソの天才だ
(男性 ：おめでとう　お幸せに)
(アビン：さよなら)
アン ：（そんなにご心配しなくても）
　　　　結婚してとは言わないわ
ジョー ：ありがたい
アン ：ホッとしすぎだわ
ジョー ：じゃ しないよ
アン ：私もウソが上手でしょ？
ジョー ：最高だ
(アビン：そのとおり)

I'm a good liar too, aren't I, Mr. Bradley?

「私もウソが上手でしょう、ね、ブラッドレーさん？」

ANN: Thank you very much.
JOE : Say... come with me!

このセリフ、会話にいただき！
- You can get away with anything.（何からでも逃れられる）の get away は「逃れる」の意味。悪いことをした相手を責めるときに You just can't get away with it.（それから逃れられないぞ）などと使う。

The best I ever met.
「最高に上手だ」
Uh-huh!
「うん！」

アン　　：ありがとう
ジョー　：そうだ　ついておいで

このニュアンスを味わう！
- **That's a hot one!**（あれは傑作だよ！）の **hot** は「素晴らしい、よくできた」の意味。**one** は lie（ウソ）のこと。

Scene 34 サンタマリア イン コスメディン教会・真実の口
「真実の口の言い伝え」

It's the Mouth of Truth.
「真実の口だ」

JOE : It's the Mouth of Truth.
　　　The legend is that if you're given to lying, you put your hand in there, it'll be bitten off.
ANN : Ooh, what a horrid idea.
JOE : Let's see you do it.
ANN : Let's see you do it.
JOE : Sure.
ANN : No! No, no, no...
JOE : Hello!
ANN : You beast!
　　　It was perfectly all right!
　　　You're not hurt!
JOE : I'm sorry, it was just a joke!
　　　All right?
ANN : You've never hurt your hand.
JOE : I'm sorry, I'm sorry. Okay?
ANN : Yes.
JOE : All right, let's go. Look out!!
ANN : Ah!

Let's see you do it.

「さあ、やってごらん」

ジョー　：“真実の口”だ
　　　　　言い伝えではウソつきが手を入れると
　　　　　食いちぎられる
アン　　：恐ろしいわね
ジョー　：試してみろよ
アン　　：あなたの番よ
ジョー　：もちろんさ
(アン　　：いや！だめ)
ジョー　：コンニチハ
アン　　：ひどいわ
　　　　　心配したのに
　　　　　大丈夫なのね
ジョー　：ごめんよ
　　　　　ただの冗談さ
アン　　：手はケガしてないのね
ジョー　：（ごめんよ　ごめん）大丈夫？
(アン　　：ええ)
ジョー　：じゃあ行こう　後ろ！

No! No, no, no...
「いや！いや、いや…」
Hello!
「コンニチワ！」

このニュアンスを味わう！
- **if you're given to lying** は「ウソをつくくせがあるなら」。**Let's see you do it.**（さあ、やってごらん）とジョーとアンが互いに言っているが、互いにウソをついているので、このシーンは緊張感がでている。

You beast!
「ひどい人！」

このトリビアで通になろう！
● ジョーが手をかくして食いちぎられたかのように演じたのはペックのアドリブだった。ヘプバーンは本当にびっくりして叫んだが、それがすごくリアルでワンテイクでOKになった。この顔の石盤はローマ時代の井戸のふたで、海神トリトーネを模したもの。「真実の口」（**The Mouth of Truth**）はイタリア語では **Le Bocca della Verita**。

Scene 35 モルガーニ通り・祈りの壁
「かなわぬ願い事」

Lovely story.
「いい話だわ」

Read some of the inscriptions.
「ちょっと読んでごらん」

- IRV : I'll park at the corner.
- ANN : What do they mean – all these inscriptions?
- JOE : Well, each one represents a wish fulfilled.
  All started during the war, when there was an air raid, right out here.
  A man with his four children was caught in the street.
  They ran over against the wall, right there, for shelter, prayed for safety.
  Bombs fell very close but no one was hurt. Later on, the man came back and he put up the first of these tablets.
  Since then it's become sort of a shrine.
  People come, and whenever their wishes are granted, they put up another one of these little plaques.
- ANN : Lovely story.
- JOE : Read some of the inscriptions.
  Make a wish? Tell the doctor?

Make a wish?
Tell the doctor?

「願いごとか？
　先生に話してごらん」

アビン　：角に停めてくる
アン　　：この文字が書かれた板は？
ジョー　：願いがかなったしるしだ
　　　　　戦時中にさかのぼるが

　　　　　子供連れの男が空襲にあった

　　　　　この壁まで逃げ込み無事を祈った

　　　　　近くを爆撃されたが
　　　　　家族は無事
　　　　　後日　彼はここに最初の板をかけた
　　　　　それ以来祈りの場所になった
　　　　　願いがかなうと
　　　　　新たな板をかける

アン　　：いい話だわ
ジョー　：読んでごらん
　　　　　願いごとか？　先生に話してごらん

Anyway, the chances of it being granted are very slight.

「どうせかないそうにもないわ」

ANN : Anyway, the chances of it being granted are very slight.
IRV : Well, what now?
ANN : I've heard of a wonderful place for dancing on a boat.
JOE : Oh, you mean the barges down by Sant'Angelo.
ANN : Yes! Couldn't we go over tonight?
IRV : Hey, why not?
JOE : Anything you wish.
ANN : And at midnight, I'll turn into a pumpkin and drive away in my glass slipper.
JOE : And that'll be the end of the fairy tale.
Well, I guess, er, Irving has to go now.
IRV : I do?
JOE : Yes, you know, that big business development of yours that you have to attend to?
IRV : Ah- oh, the development!
JOE : Yes, can't afford not to take care of that.
IRV : Yeah. Er, I'll, er, see you later, Smitty.

I've heard of a wonderful place for dancing on a boat.

「船の上でダンスができる素敵な場所があるんですって」

アン　　：どうせかないそうにもないわ

アビン　：お次は何だ？
アン　　：船上でダンスがあると

ジョー　：サンタンジェロだな
アン　　：今夜 行かない？
アビン　：いいね
ジョー　：君の望みとあれば
アン　　：でも12時になると
　　　　　カボチャの馬車でいなくなる
ジョー　：それで おとぎ話はおしまいだな
　　　　　そろそろ 彼は帰る時間だ
アビン　：何でだ？
ジョー　：ネガわくば大仕事に
　　　　　専念してもらいたい
アビン　：あの仕事か
ジョー　：やらないとね
アビン　：また後で会おう　スミッティ

And at midnight, I'll turn into a pumpkin and drive away in my glass slipper.

「そして真夜中にかぼちゃに変身してガラスの靴で去ってしまうの」

ANN : Good luck with the big development.
IRV : Yeah, thanks.

このニュアンスを味わう!
● **Make a wish?** は **Did you make a wish?**（願い事した？）。**Tell the doctor?**（先生に言ってみる？）はジョーがアンの世話をする先生（医者）のような感じでたずねている。

このセリフ、会話にいただき!
● **Well, what now?**（さあ、これからどうする？）は簡単で便利な表現。次に何をするかをたずねるときにもってこい。**Now what?** と言うと「あれっ、どうしたんだ？」。

Yes, you know, that big business development of yours that you have to attend to?
「そう、ネガわくば大仕事に専念してもらいたい」

アン　　：大仕事がんばって

このニュアンスを味わう!
- **Anything you wish.**（お望みなら何でも）は、アンの Anyway, the chances of it being granted are very slight.（願いがかなえられる見込みはほとんどないわ）を受けた言葉。ジョーの心優しさが表れている。

このダブル・ミーニングでにやり!
- **development** には「開発」のほか「写真の現像」の意味もあり、ジョーはアンにわからないように big business development と言って「大きな仕事の開発」と「写真の現像」とをかけている。「ネガわくば大仕事に専念してもらいたい」という感じ。

Scene 36

サンタンジェロ城下の船
「パーティでの大騒動」

I think you are a ringer.
「あなたは"クリソツ"だと思うわ」

JOE : Grazie.

ANN : Hello.
JOE : Hello.
ANN : Mr. Bradley, if you don't mind my saying so, I-I think you are a ringer.
JOE : Oh- wha-? Oh, thanks very much.
ANN : You've spent the whole day doing things I've always wanted to. Why?
JOE : I don't know. Seemed the thing to do.
ANN : I've never heard of anybody so kind.
JOE : Wasn't any trouble.
ANN : Or so completely unselfish.
JOE : Let's have a drink at the bar.

MAR : Oh! Finalmente! There you are!
Er, scusatemi tanto. I look for you a long time.
I think maybe you not come. Ah, off, all off!
ANN : Oh, it's nice without, isn't it? Cool.

Hit him again, Smitty!
「もう1回やって!」

アン　　：こんにちは
ジョー　：こんにちは
アン　　：あなたは とても "クリソツ" だと思うわ
ジョー　：何だって?
　　　　　それは どうもありがとう
アン　　：私のために丸一日
　　　　　付き合ってくれるなんて
ジョー　：そうすべきって感じで
アン　　：こんなに親切な方はいませんわ
ジョー　：たいしたことないよ
アン　　：よっぽど寛容な方ね
ジョー　：バーで何か飲もう

マリオ　：やっと会えた　ここに来ていたんだね
　　　　　ずっと捜してた　もう来ないのかと
　　　　　全部そった
アン　　：ヒゲがないほうが素敵ね

MAR : Oh, very, very good.
ANN : This is Mr. Bradley.
MAR : I, Mario Delani.
JOE : Old friends?
ANN : Oh, yes, he cut my hair this afternoon. He invited me here tonight.
JOE : Wha- what did you say the name was?
MAR : Delani – Mario Delani.
JOE : Mario Delani.
MAR : Yes.
JOE : I'm very glad to know you.
MAR : Me, too. Oh, may I enjoy myself, er, the pleasure? You mind?
JOE : No, no – go right ahead.
MAR : Thank you.

IRV : Stampa! Ciao, Joe. Did I miss anything?
JOE : You're just in time, pal.
IRV : Who's Smitty dancing with?
JOE : Barber – cut her hair this afternoon, made a date for tonight.
IRV : 'The Princess and the barber'.

ANN : What is it?
MAR : Moment.
MAN : August!
MAR : Oh. Thank you. Bye.

MAN : Your Highness.
You will dance quietly towards the entrance.
There's a car waiting.

マリオ　：とてもいい感じ
アン　　：こちらブラッドレーさん
マリオ　：マリオ・ディラーニ
ジョー　：古い知り合い？
アン　　：美容師さんよ
　　　　　ここに誘ってくれたの
ジョー　：お名前をもう一度
マリオ　：マリオ・ディラーニ
ジョー　：マリオ・ディラーニさんね
(マリオ：そうです)
ジョー　：どうぞよろしく
マリオ　：こちらこそ
　　　　　彼女と踊りたいのですがいいですか？
ジョー　：どうぞ
マリオ　：ありがとう

アビン　：いいネタあった？
ジョー　：いい所に来た
アビン　：踊ってるのは？
ジョー　：床屋だって
　　　　　髪を切ってデートの約束を
アビン　："王女と床屋"か

アン　　：どうかした？
マリオ　：待てよ
男性　　：オーギュスト
マリオ　：ありがとう
　　　　　それじゃ
男性　　：王女様
　　　　　このまま出口へ
　　　　　車を待たせてあります

ANN : No...
MAN : Your Highness, please!
ANN : You...you've made a mistake.
I non parlo Inglese. Let me go!
Will you let me go? Mr. Bradley!
Let me go, will you? Mr. Bradley!
IRV : Hit him again, Smitty!
Joe, give me my car keys.
JOE : Police! Police!
IRV : Come on, the other side of the bridge!

このニュアンスを味わう!
- アンが I think you are a ringer.(あなたはとても"クリソツ"だと思うわ)と言ったのは、ringer を「とても魅力的な人」という意味と思っているため。ジョーに恋心を抱いている。アンの初恋。
- アンはジョーの気持ちを聞きたくて質問するが、彼はやましさを感じており、アンの純粋な心をもてあそぶことができない。そこで Seemed the thing to do.(そうすべきって感じだった)や Wasn't any trouble.(大したことじゃない)とそっけなく答える。そして Let's have a drink at the bar.(バーで一杯飲もう)と言ってその話を止める。
- Let me go!(はなして!)の let には「希望どおりにさせてあげて」というニュアンスがある。Will you let me go?(どうかはなして)の Will には「強い依頼」が感じられる。

アン	：イヤよ
男性	：王女様
アン	：人違いですわ
	（英語は話しません）
	放してくださらない？
	放してちょうだい　ブラッドレーさん　助けて
アビン	：もう1回
	車の鍵だ
ジョー	：警察だ
アビン	：橋の反対側へ

このセリフ、会話にいただき！
- **Did I miss anything?**（何か逃がしたかな？）は、パーティや会合に遅れてきたときなどに使える。この miss は「取り逃がす、つかみそこねる」といった感じ。
- **You're just in time.**（ちょうど間に合ったよ）は日常会話でそのまま使える。**You came at the perfect time.**（ちょうどいい時に来たよ）も覚えておきたい。

このイタリア語がわかればもっと楽しめる！
- **I non parlo Inglese.**（私は英語を話しません）とアンはイタリア語で言っている。**Parlo** は **I speak** で、**Inglese**は **English**。**Parlo Inglese.** なら「英語を話します」で、**Parli Inglese?** なら「英語を話しますか？」。

Scene 37

テヴェレ川・橋の下のアーチ
「ジョーとアン王女の初めてのキス」

Say, you know, you were great back there.
「ねえ、君、あそこでは大活躍だったね」

JOE : All right?
ANN : Fine. How are you?
JOE : Oh, fine!
　　　Say, you know, you were great back there.
ANN : You weren't so bad yourself.

JOE : Well...I...I guess we'd better get Irving's car, and get out of here.

このニュアンスを味わう!
● **You weren't so bad yourself.** は「まんざら悪くなかった」だが「なかなかよかった」というニュアンス。食べ物などについても **Not bad.** や **Not bad at all.** などと使う。

You weren't so bad yourself.
「あなたもなかなかだったわ」

ジョー　：大丈夫か？
アン　　：あなたこそ
ジョー　：大丈夫だとも
　　　　　さっきの君は すごかった
アン　　：あなたも なかなかだったわ

ジョー　：そろそろ行ったほうがよさそうだ

このニュアンスを味わう！
● I guess we'd better get Irving's car, and get out of here. は「アービングの車に乗ってここから離れたほうがいい」という意味。had better... は「…しなければ問題が起きる」というニュアンスがある。

Scene 38 ジョーのアパート・室内
「ジョーとアン王女の心中」

Everything ruined?
「全部 台無し？」
No...they'll be dry in a minute.
「いいえ…すぐに乾くわ」

RAD : This is the American Hour from Rome, continuing our program of musical selections.

JOE : Everything ruined?
ANN : No...they'll be dry in a minute.
JOE : Suits you.
You should always wear my clothes.
ANN : Seems I do.
JOE : I thought a little wine might be good.
ANN : Shall I cook something?
JOE : No kitchen.
Nothing to cook, I always eat out.
ANN : Do you like that?
JOE : Well, life isn't always what one likes, is it?
ANN : No, it isn't.

JOE : Tired?
ANN : A little.
JOE : You've had quite a day.

Well, life isn't always what one likes, is it?
「人生はままならないからね、そうだろ?」

No, it isn't.
「ええ、そうね」

ラジオ ：引き続き音楽番組を
　　　　お楽しみください

ジョー ：全部 台無し？
アン 　：いいえ　すぐに乾くわ
ジョー ：僕の服が似合うね
　　　　（いつも着てたら）
アン 　：そうね
ジョー ：少し飲むといいかな
アン 　：何か作りましょうか？
ジョー ：台所がない
　　　　いつも外食ばかりだ
アン 　：それが好きなの？
ジョー ：人生は ままならない　そうだろ？
アン 　：ええ　そうね

ジョー ：疲れた？
アン 　：少しね
ジョー ：大変な１日だったね

173

I...have to go now.
「もう…行かなくては」

ANN : A wonderful day!
RAD : This is the American Hour from Rome, broadcasting a special news bulletin in English and Italian.
Tonight, there is no further word from the bedside of Princess Ann in Rome, where she was taken ill yesterday on the last leg of her European goodwill tour.
This has given rise to rumors that her condition may be serious, which is causing alarm and anxiety among the people in her country.
La Principessa Anna...

ANN : The news can wait till tomorrow.
JOE : Yes.
ANN : May I have a little more wine?
I'm sorry I couldn't cook us some dinner.
JOE : Did you learn how in school?
ANN : Mmmm, I'm a good cook.

Anya...there's... something that I want to tell you...

「アーニャ…君に…話しておくことがある…」

アン　　：でも楽しかった
ラジオ　：番組からニュースを
　　　　　お知らせいたします

　　　　　昨夜 病気に倒れた
　　　　　アン王女のその後の容体は
　　　　　まだ知らされておりません

　　　　　病状悪化のうわさもあり
　　　　　母国にも懸念の色が
　　　　　広がっています
　　　　　(アン王女は…)

アン　　：明日でいいわ
ジョー　：そうだな
アン　　：もっとお酒を
　　　　　料理ができなくて残念
ジョー　：学校で習った？
アン　　：料理の腕はプロも顔負けなのよ

ANN : I could earn my living at it.
I can sew too, and clean a house, and iron.
I learned to do all those things.
I just...haven't had the chance to do it for anyone.
JOE : Well, looks like I'll have to move...and get myself a place with a kitchen.
ANN : Yes.
I...have to go now.

JOE : Anya...there's...something that I want to tell you...
ANN : No, please...nothing.
I must go and get dressed.

このニュアンスを味わう!
- アパートの前のワンカットに注目。ジョーとアンが2人だけの時間を持った(結ばれた)という間接的な表現。ジョーが Everything ruined?(服はみんなダメ?)と聞いたのに対してアンが No... they'll be dry in a minute.(いいえ、すぐに乾くわ)と答えているのは服が乾くまで2人だけの時間があったことの暗示。
- Suits you. You should always wear my clothes.(似合うよ。僕の服をいつも着るといい)は「僕たち、これからどうする」ということを間接的にたずねたもの。

アン	：（料理で食べていけるわ） 　　お裁縫も アイロンがけも 　　何でも一通り習ったわ 　　ただ披露する機会がなくて
ジョー	：どうやら台所付きの家に 　　引っ越したほうがよさそうだ
アン	：そうね 　　もう行かなくては
ジョー	：君に話しておくことがある
アン	：言わないで今は何も 　　着替えてくるわ

このニュアンスを味わう!

- Well, looks like I'll have to move...and get myself a place with a kitchen.（じゃ、引っ越すしかないかな…台所のある部屋を見つけて）も「僕たち、これからどうする」という意味。それに対して、I...have to go now.（もう、帰らなければ）とアンは別れることを決心して言う。
- Anya...there's...something that I want to tell you... は「アーニャ、君をだますのはいやで、本当のことを言いたい」というジョーの言葉に対してアンは「愛してる」と言われると思って No, please...nothing. とさえぎる。

Scene 39　アービングの車の中
「ジョーとアン王女の切ない別れ」

Stop at the next corner, please.
「次の角で停めて」
Okay.
「分かった」

- ANN : Stop at the next corner, please.
- JOE : Okay.
  Here?
- ANN : Yes. I have to leave you now.
  I'm going to that corner there, and turn.
  You must stay in the car and drive away.
  Promise not to watch me go beyond the corner.
  Just drive away and leave me, as I leave you.
- JOE : All right.
- ANN : I don't know how to say goodbye.
  I can't think of any words.
- JOE : Don't try.

このニュアンスを味わう!
- I have to leave you now...Just drive away and leave me, as I leave you. 「初恋の人」で「初めての男」にもう2度と会えない。アンが高まる感情をおさえて、やっと言った言葉。非常に切なくて泣けてくる。

Just drive away and leave me, as I leave you.

「ただ車を走らせて、私を置いたままで、私もお別れします」

アン　　：次の角で停めて
ジョー　：分かった
　　　　　ここ？
アン　　：ええ　お別れしないと
　　　　　私は　あそこの角を曲がるけど
　　　　　車から下りないでね
　　　　　あの角から先は見ないと約束して
　　　　　ただ車を走らせて私を置いたままで私もお別れします
ジョー　：分かった
アン　　：何とお別れを言えば
　　　　　言葉が思いつかなくて
ジョー　：無理しなくても

このニュアンスを味わう!

● アンが **I don't know how to say goodbye. I can't think of any words.**（なんてお別れを言えばいいのかわからない。言葉が思いつかないの）と言えば、**Don't try.**（無理しなくていいよ）と答える。そのあと、本当に切ない気持ちがこみ上げてくる。

Scene 40

大使館・アン王女の寝室
「威厳のあるアン王女」

...twenty-four hours...they can't all be blank.

「…24時間を丸々空白にはできません」

AMB : Your Royal Highness...twenty-four hours...they can't all be blank.
ANN : They are not.
AMB : But what explanation am I to offer Their Majesties?
ANN : I was indisposed. I am better.
AMB : Ma'am — you must appreciate that I have my duty to perform, just as Your Royal Highness has Her duty...
ANN : Your Excellency, I trust you will not find it necessary to use that word again.
Were I not completely aware of my duty to my family and my country, I would not have come tonight. Or indeed, ever again.
Now, since I understand we have a very full schedule today, you have my permission to withdraw.
No milk and crackers.
That will be all, thank you, Countess.

I was indisposed. I am better.

「具合が悪くなり、回復したのです」

大使　：王女様
　　　　24時間を丸々空白にはできません
アン　：そうね
大使　：両陛下には何と申し開きを？

アン　：病気だったが　回復したと
大使　：自覚してくださいまし
　　　　私に義務があるのと同じく
　　　　王女様にも義務があるのです
アン　：閣下　そのお言葉はもう必要ありません

　　　　王家と国家に対する義務を自覚してなければ
　　　　今夜 戻ることはなく
　　　　それどころか二度とは
　　　　今日の日程はいっぱいですね
　　　　もう下がってよろしい

　　　　ミルクも結構
　　　　もういいわ　ご苦労様

I trust you will not find it necessary to use that word again.

「そのお言葉はもう
 必要ないと存じます」

このニュアンスを味わう!
● I trust you will not find it necessary to use that word again.（2度とその言葉をお使いになる必要はないと確信します）でアンは王女として威厳と権威に満ちている。**that word** は **duty**（義務）のこと。

No milk and crackers.

「ミルクとクラッカーは要りません」

このニュアンスを味わう!
- Were I not completely aware of my duty... は仮定法で、条件節が倒置されている。If I were not... と同じだが、倒置のほうが仮定ということが強調される。
- 初めは子供っぽい娘だったのが、ここでは黒い服を着ていかにも大人になった感じ。側仕えに毅然とした態度でのぞむ。No milk and crackers. もアンが大人の女性になったことを示す（→20ページ）。

Scene 41　ジョーのアパート・室内
「支局長のジョーへの追及」

Where is that story?
「記事はどこだ？」
I have no story.
「ありません」

HEN :　Joe, is it true?
　　　　Did you really get it?
JOE :　Did I get what?
HEN :　The Princess story, the exclusive!
　　　　Did you get it?
JOE :　No, no, I didn't get it.
HEN :　What? But that's impossible!
JOE :　Have a cup of coffee or something?
HEN :　Joe, you can't hold out on me.
JOE :　Who's holding out on you?
HEN :　You are.
JOE :　What are you talking about?
HEN :　I know too much!
　　　　First you come into my office and ask about an exclusive on the Princess.
　　　　Next, you disappear, then I get the rumor from my contact at the Embassy that the Princess isn't sick at all and she's out on the town.

Irving!
「アービング!」
What's the idea?!
「何のつもりだ」

支局長　：（本当か？）
　　　　　手に入れたか？
ジョー　：何をです？
支局長　：独占インタビューだよ
　　　　　（手に入れたか？）
ジョー　：ダメでした
支局長　：そんなはずない
ジョー　：コーヒーは？
支局長　：隠し立てできんぞ
ジョー　：誰がです？
支局長　：君がだよ
（ジョー：何の話です？）
支局長　：分かってるぞ
　　　　　独占記事の提案の後
　　　　　君はいなくなった
　　　　　大使館から
　　　　　王女失踪のうわさも聞いた
　　　　　（病気じゃなく町にでてると）

JOE : What kind of a newspaper man are you?
You believe every two-bit rumor that comes your way?

HEN : Yeah. And a lot of other rumors - about a shindig at a barge down by the river and the arrest of eight secret service men from a country which shall be nameless.
And then comes the news of the lady's miraculous recovery. It all adds up!
And don't think by playing hard-to-get you're going to raise the price on that story.
A deal's a deal! Now, come on, come on, come on.
Where is that story?

JOE : I have no story.

HEN : Then what was the idea of...

IRV : Joe! Man, wait till you see these!

JOE : Irving...

IRV : Hiya, Mr. Henne— oh, you got here at the right time.
Wait till you get a look at...

JOE : Irving!

IRV : What's the idea?!

JOE : What do you mean, charging in and spilling things all over my place!

IRV : Who's spilling?

JOE : You did! I spoke to you about that once before. Don't you remember?

IRV : Joe, look at my pants!

JOE : Yeah, you better come in here and dry them off, Irving.

ジョー　：うわさをいちいち
　　　　　本気にするんですか？

支局長　：ほかにもある
　　　　　川でのパーティーのこと
　　　　　某国の調査団が
　　　　　8人拘束されたこと
　　　　　それに王女が奇跡的に回復したこと
　　　　　すべてつじつまが合う
　　　　　値段を吊り上げるつもりか
　　　　　約束は約束だ
　　　　　今すぐ出せ
　　　　　記事はどこだ

ジョー　：ありません
支局長　：それじゃ…
アビン　：ジョー　これを見てみろよ
（ジョー：アービング）
アビン　：どうも
　　　　　支局長さん
　　　　　（ちょうどいい所に…）
（ジョー：アービング）
アビン　：何すんだよ
ジョー　：また君は こぼしたのか
　　　　　（僕の部屋中に！）
アビン　：誰がだよ
ジョー　：気をつけろと言ったのに
　　　　　（忘れたのか？）
アビン　：これ見ろよ
ジョー　：こっちで乾かせ

That's all there is to it. There is no story.

「ただそれだけのことですよ。
記事はありません」

IRV : Aww, nuts to that.
Hey, did you tell him about Smitty?
JOE : Irving...
HEN : Smitty?
IRV : Oh ho! Mr. Hennessy, wait till you...
JOE : There you go again, Irving!
IRV : Joe...Listen, th...
JOE : Hey, all right, save that till later.
You're here early anyway.
Why don't you go home and shave!
IRV : Shave?
JOE : Yeah, or else keep quiet till Mr. Hennessy and I are finished talking.
HEN : Hey, what kind of a routine is that?
What are you guys up to?
Who's Smitty?
JOE : Oh, he's a guy that we met.
You wouldn't care for him...
HEN : What am I supposed to look at?

Same time, same place. Maybe that's one story you can get!

「同じ時間、同じ場所だ。
取れる記事はそれぐらい
だろう！」

アビン　：それよりスミッティの話はした？

（ジョー　：おい…）
支局長　：スミッティって？
（アビン　：支局長　これを…）
ジョー　：アービングってば　またやったな
（アビン　：聞いてくれ…）
ジョー　：ひとまず後にしろ
　　　　　　（早く来すぎだ）
　　　　　今は家に戻ってヒゲをそれ
アビン　：ヒゲを？
ジョー　：話が終わるまで
　　　　　黙っててくれ
支局長　：一体 何の話をしている
　　　　　スミッティって誰だ

ジョー　：知り合った男です
　　　　　（ご興味はないと…）
支局長　：中身は？

JOE : Oh, just a couple of Irving's dames.
　　　　You, you wouldn't like them.
　　　　Er, maybe you would...
HEN : Don't change the subject!
　　　　When you came back into my office yesterday...
JOE : Yeah, I know, yesterday at noon I thought I had a good lead, but I was wrong!
　　　　That's all there is to it.
　　　　There is no story.
HEN : Okay. She's holding the press interview today.
　　　　Same time, same place.
　　　　Maybe that's one story you can get!
　　　　And you owe me five hundred bucks!
JOE : Take it out of my salary.
　　　　Fifty bucks a week.
HEN : Don't think I won't!

このニュアンスを味わう！
- Joe, you can't hold out on me.（ジョー、隠そうとしたってそうはいかんぞ）のなかの hold out は「情報などを隠す、与えない」という意味。hold out on someone で「人に隠し事をする」。
- two-bit は「おそまつな、安っぽい、つまらない」の意味。two-bit rumor（つまらないうわさ）を信じるなんてとジョーは支局長の追及をかわそうとしている。

このダブル・ミーニングでにやり！
- spilling things all over my place!（人の部屋中に物をこぼして！）とジョーはここでも spill の「（液体などを）こぼす」に「（秘密などを）もらす」の意味をかけている。
- Why don't you go home and shave!（家に帰ってヒゲでもそったらどうだ！）でジョーは「ヒゲをそる」のshaveにclose shave（危機一髪）をかけている。

ジョー	：女の写真です
	きっとお気に召さない
	もしかして…
支局長	：話をそらすな
	昨日の口ぶりでは…
ジョー	：確かに昨日は
	あてがあった
	でも外れたんです
	記事はありません
支局長	：分かった
	今日また記者会見が開かれる
	記事を取ってこい
	500ドルの貸しだぞ
ジョー	：天引きしてください
	（週50ドル）
支局長	：当たり前だ

このセリフ、会話にいただき！

- It all adds up!（すべてつじつまが合う）の add up は「すべて足し合わせてみて、ぴったり合う」ということで、話や行動の「つじつまが合う」「筋がとおる」という意味。It adds up all right.（筋はちゃんと通っている）、It just doesn't add up.（つじつまが合わない）などと使う。
- What are you guys up to? は「君たち何をたくらんでるんだ？」。この up to は「たくらむ、もくろむ」で「取り組み」という意味もある。What are you up to? なら「何に取り組んでいるの？」。
- That's all there is to it. は「それだけの話」という意味で、会話でよく使われる。

Scene 42 ジョーのアパート・室内
「アン王女の写真」

You wanna have a look at 'em?
「写真を見たいだろう?」

IRV : Hey, what gives?
　　　Have we had a better offer?
JOE : Irving...I, I don't know just how to tell you this, but...
IRV : Wait till I sit down.
JOE : Well, in regard to the story...that goes with these... there is no story.
IRV : W-why not?
JOE : I mean, not as far as I'm concerned.
IRV : Er, well, the, er, pictures came out pretty well. You want to have a look at them?
　　　Huh? How about a blow-up from a negative that size, huh?
JOE : Yeah. Ha, that's her first cigarette, huh?
IRV : Oh yeah, at Rocca's.
　　　Hey, the Mouth of Truth.
　　　Oh, you want to know the caption I had in mind there?
　　　'Barber cuts in' — huh?

Hey, the Mouth of Truth.
「ほら、真実の口だ」

アビン　：どうした？
　　　　　ほかにいい条件が？
ジョー　：どう説明すればいいのか

アビン　：座らせてくれ
ジョー　：記事のことだが
　　　　　この写真につける記事はない
アビン　：何でだ？
ジョー　：つまり 僕としてはだ
アビン　：写真は うまくできたよ
　　　　　ちょっと見るかい？
　　　　　このネガから引き伸ばしたのに

ジョー　：初めてのタバコ
アビン　：（ロッカでだ）
　　　　　ほら、真実の口だ
　　　　　見出しも浮かんだよ
　　　　　"床屋 カットイン"

193

'The Wall Where Wishes Come True'

「願いがかなう壁」

JOE : Well, here's the one I figured — would be the key shot for the whole layout.
'The Wall Where Wishes Come True', hmm?
IRV : Joe, that's good!
Lead off with that, then follow up with the wishes?
JOE : Yeah.
IRV : I dug that up out of a file.
'Princess Inspects Police'.
JOE : Yeah, but...
IRV : 'Police Inspects Princess'. Huh?
How about that?
JOE : Yeah. Pretty good, pretty good.
IRV : Oh, wait Joe, I got topper for you - there.
JOE : Wow!
IRV : Is that a shot!
JOE : What a picture!
IRV : Is that a shot, Joe!
'Body Guard Gets Body Blow!'

Is that a shot!
「すごいだろ！」
What a picture!
「すごい写真だ！」

ジョー　：これは記事の中心になるな
　　　　　　"願いがかなう壁"
　　　　　（どうだ？）
アビン　：いいね
　　　　　それに続けて
　　　　　願いの写真を入れる
（ジョー：そうだな）
アビン　：こんな写真があった
　　　　　　"王女 警察をご視察"
（ジョー：いいね　だが…）
アビン　："警察 王女の取り調べ"
　　　　　どうだよ？
ジョー　：これは面白いな
（アビン：傑作があるんだ）
（ジョー：すごい！）
アビン　：すごいだろ！
ジョー　：やったな
アビン　：傑作だろう？
　　　　　　"ボディガードのボディに一発"

JOE : Yeah. No, no, how about this?
'Crowned Head' – huh?
IRV : Oh, I get it! That... Joe, you got...
She's fair game, Joe.
It's always open season on princesses.
You must be out of your mind!
JOE : Yeah, I know, but, er, look I can't prevent you from selling the pictures, if you want to.
You'll get a good price for them.
IRV : Yeah!
JOE : You going to the interview?
IRV : You going?
JOE : Yeah. Well, it's an assignment, isn't it?
IRV : Yeah. I'll see you.

このセリフ、会話にいただき！
- What gives? は俗語で「どうしたんだ？」「なにごとだ？」という意味で、What's up? と同じ。親しい人に使う。両方ともあいさつとして「どうしてる？」と使うことも多い。
- The pictures came out pretty well. （写真はよく撮れてたよ）というのは日常会話でそのまま使える。come out は「写真がはっきり写っている」。

ジョー	：それよりもこれは？ "王冠をかぶった頭"
アビン	：それだ うまいこと言う 彼女は格好のネタだ いつ食らいついてもいいんだ 気は確かか？
ジョー	：分かってるけど… 君が写真を売るなら邪魔はしない いい値がつくぞ
(アビン	：ああ！)
ジョー	：記者会見には？
アビン	：行くのか？
ジョー	：ああ 仕事だからな
アビン	：また後で

このニュアンスを味わう！

- I got topper for you - there.（傑作があるんだ、ほら）の topper は「いちばん上のもの」ということで「すぐれた人や物」を指す。
- Is that a shot! は疑問文ではなく強調文。「すごい写真だろ！」というニュアンス。それにジョーは What a picture! と感嘆文で答えている。「なんてすごい写真だ！」。「ローマの休日」は、What a movie!（なんてすごい映画だ！）と言える。
- fair game は「格好の獲物」で、open season は「狩猟期」。She's fair game, Joe. It's always open season on princesses. は「彼女は格好のネタだ、ジョー。王女様たちにはいつ食らいついてもいいんだ」という感じ。

Scene 43 大使館・応接室
「アン王女の記者会見」

I am in favor of any measure which would lead to closer cooperation in Europe.

「欧州の緊密化促進策なら すべて賛成です」

- IRV : It ain't much, but it's home.
- NOB : Ladies and Gentlemen, please approach.
- MAJ : Sua Altezza Reale – Her Royal Highness.
- AMB : Your Royal Highness – the ladies and gentlemen of the press.
- M.C. : Ladies and gentlemen, Her Royal Highness will now answer your questions.
- PRS : I believe at the outset, Your Highness, that I should express the pleasure of all of us at your recovery from the recent illness.
- ANN : Thank you.
- FRN : Does Your Highness believe that federation would be a possible solution to Europe's economic problems?
- ANN : I am in favor of any measure which would lead to closer cooperation in Europe.
- ITA : And what, in the opinion of Your Highness, is the outlook for friendship among nations?

I have every faith in it – as I have faith in relations between people.

「国家間の友好を心から信じます、人と人との友情と同じく」

アビン　：これが家か　たいしたことない
式部官　：皆様 こちらへどうぞ
執事長　：王女様のお出ましです
大使　　：王女様　こちらが
　　　　　記者の方々です
式部官　：これから皆様のご質問に
　　　　　お答えします
米記者　：最初に 一同を代表して
　　　　　先のご病気からのご回復
　　　　　お喜び申し上げます
アン　　：感謝いたします
仏記者　：欧州の連邦化が
　　　　　経済問題の解決策だと
　　　　　ご自身もお考えですか
アン　　：欧州の緊密化促進の
　　　　　政策であれば賛成です
伊記者　：国家間の友好関係について
　　　　　今後の見通しは どうですか？

> **we believe that Your Highness' faith will not be unjustified.**
> 「王女様のご信頼が裏切られることはないでしょう」

ANN : I have every faith in it — as I have faith in relations between people.
JOE : May I say, speaking from my own press service, we believe that Your Highness' faith will not be unjustified.
ANN : I am so glad to hear you say it.
SWE : Which of the cities visited did Your Highness enjoy the most?
GEN : "Each in its own way..."
ANN : Each in its own way was...unforgettable.
It would be difficult to... Rome!
By all means, Rome!
I will cherish my visit here in memory as long as I live.
GER : Despite your indisposition, Your Highness?
ANN : Despite that.

M.C. : Photographs may now be taken.
AMB : Thank you, ladies and gentlemen.

Rome! By all means, Rome! I will cherish my visit here in memory as long as I live.

「ローマです！何と申してもローマです！ 私はここを訪れたことを想い出として生涯いつくしみます」

アン	：友好を心から信じます
	人と人との友情と同じく
ジョー	：わが社を代表して申し上げます
	王女様のご信頼は裏切られないでしょう
アン	：それをうかがい大変嬉しく思います
ス記者	：訪問地でどこが一番
	お気に召しましたか？
将軍	：それぞれ…
アン	：それぞれ忘れがたい思い出があります
	とても1つには…ローマです
	何と申してもローマです
	この地の思い出は一生大切にします
独記者	：ご病気になられたのに？
アン	：そうです
式部官	：写真撮影の時間です
大使	：本日はどうも

AMB : Thank you very much.

ANN : I would now like to meet some of the ladies and gentlemen of the press.

PRS : Hitchcock, Chicago Daily News.
ANN : I am so happy to see you, Mr. Hitchcock.
PRS : Thank you.
SCA : Scanziani de La Suisse.
KLI : Klinger, Deutsche Presse Agentur.
ANN : Freut mich sehr!
MON : Maurice Montaberis, Le Figaro.
GAL : Sytske Galema of De Line, Amsterdam.
ANN : Dag, mevrouw.
FER : Jacques Ferris, Ici Paris.
ANN : Enchantee.
GRS : Gross, Davar Tel Aviv.
CAV : Cortes Cavanillas, ABC Madrid.
ANN : Encantande!
LAM : Lampe, New York Herald Tribune.
ANN : Good afternoon.
LAM : Good afternoon.
IRV : Irving Radovich, C.R. Photo Service.
ANN : How do you do?
IRV : Er, may I present Your Highness with some commemorative photos of your visit to Rome?
ANN : Thank you so very much.
JOE : Joe Bradley, American News Service.
ANN : So happy, Mr. Bradley.
MOR : Moriones, La Vangurdia, Barcelona.

大使	：ありがとうございました
アン	：記者の皆様に 　ごあいさつを
米記者	：ヒッチコックです
アン	：お会いできて光栄です
(米記者	：ありがとうございます)
スカン	：スカンジアーニです
クリン	：クリンガーです
(アン	：光栄です)
モンタ	：モーリス・モンタブレです
ハレマ	：シスケ・ハレマと申します
アン	：こんにちは
フェリ	：ジャック・フェリです
(アン	：光栄です)
グロス	：グロスでございます
カバァ	：コルテス・カバニージャスです
(アン	：光栄です)
ランペ	：ランペと申します
アン	：ごきげんよう
(ランペ	：ごきげんよう)
アビン	：アービング・ラドヴィッチです
アン	：はじめまして
アビン	：お渡ししたいものが 　ローマ訪問の記念写真です
アン	：感謝いたします
ジョー	：ジョー・ブラドレーです
アン	：嬉しく思います
モリオ	：モリオネスです

HSE : Stephen House, The London Exchange Telegraph.
ANN : Good afternoon.
DEA : De Aldisio, Agent de Presse.

このニュアンスを味わう!

● アービングは応接室を見て It ain't much, but it's home.（大したことはないが、家だね）と逆のことを言っている。ain't は amn't, aren't, isn't, haven't, hasn't の代わりに使われるが標準的ではない。I ain't going. と言えば「オレは行かないよ」。

● I am in favor of any measure... の in favor of は「賛成する、支持する」という意味。硬い表現なので日常会話ではあまり使われない。

● I have every faith in it - as I have faith in relations between people.（国と国の友好を心から信じます、人と人との友情を信じるように）とアン王女はジョーに直接訴えかける。ジョーは We believe that Your Highness' faith will not be unjustified.（王女様のご信頼が裏切られることはないと確信します）と安心させる。2重否定に注目。王女が目を潤ませながら言う I am so glad to hear you say it. は情感あふれる。

ハウス　：スティーブン・ハウスです

アン　　：ごきげんよう
アルデ　：デ・アルディシオです

このニュアンスを味わう！
- 王女は無難な答えをやめて、Rome! By all means, Rome! I will cherish my visit here, in memory, as long as I live. と万感の思いを込めた言葉を叫ぶ。
- ジョーはどうにか微笑みながら Joe Bradley, American News Service. と自己紹介。アンは儀礼的に握手をしながら So happy, Mr. Bradley. (嬉しく思います。ブラッドレーさん)。非常につらくて切ない最後の別れ。

このトリビアで通になろう！
- 記者会見のシーンでは本物の記者たちが出演した。
- 「ローマの休日」はイタリアですべて撮影・製作された初のアメリカ映画。

「ローマの休日」の名所ガイド
有名シーンはここで撮影！

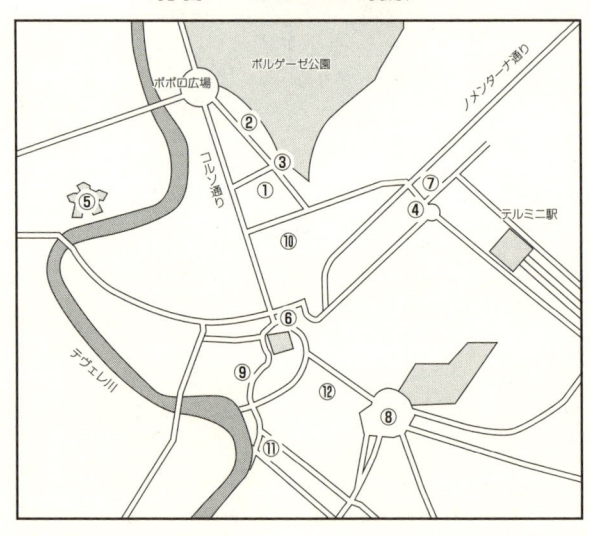

①カフェ・グレコ
②マルグッタ通り
③スペイン階段
④共和国広場
⑤サンタンジェロ城
⑥ベネチア広場
⑦バルベニーニ宮殿
⑧コロッセオ
⑨祈りの壁
⑩トレビの泉
⑪真実の口
⑫フォロロマーノ

第2部

「ローマの休日」のリスニング
発音の変化7つの公式

第2部 「ローマの休日」のリスニング
発音の変化7つの公式

● **英語の音は七変化する** ●

　日本人はなぜネイティブが話す自然な英語が聞き取れないのでしょう？　つづりを見れば知っている英語でも聞き取れないのはなぜでしょう？　それは実際の会話では英語の音はいろいろと変化するからです。

　まずは日本語の音変化を考えてみましょう。読者は、ふつうに話される日本語なら不自由なく聞き取れるはずです。たとえば

「ったく。困っちゃうな」と言われて
「まったく。困ってしまうな」

とわかります。「まったく」の「ま」が省略されていても、また、「しまう」が「ちまう」から「ちゃう」と変化しても理解できます。もっと例をあげましょう。

ってことは（ということは）
やなこった（いやなことだ）

そうだっつうの (そうだっていうの)

　このように話し言葉は、語を省略したり、短くしたり、2つの語をつなぎあわせたりして言いやすいように発音が変化するものです。

　その発音の変化が特に激しいのが英語です。実際の英語の発音は、個々の単語が発音されるときとは違っていろいろと変化します。それは英語のリズムが関係しているからです。
　ここでは、英語の発音の変化を7つの公式にしてまとめて紹介します。この知識があるだけでも「ローマの休日」がかなり聞き取れるようになります。

第1公式　音が弱くなる「弱化」

　英語では、すべての音がはっきりと発音されるわけではなく、弱くなる音があります。弱くなって消えることもあります。音が弱くなることを**弱化**（じゃくか）といいます。

●音が弱くなる例―1

　　　　トゥ ヒム　　　　　　　トゥ イム
　I spoke to him.　→　I spoke to 'im.
＊him はふつうは「ヒム」のように発音されるが、音

が弱くなって先頭の [h] が落ちる
* to 'im とつながり「トゥイム」のようになる

●音が弱くなる例―2

ワッツ ハー　　　　　　　　**ワッツアー**

<u>What's her</u> name?　→　<u>What's'er name?</u>

* her はふつうは「ハー」のように発音されるが、音が弱くなって先頭の [h] が落ちる
* What's'er とつながり「ワッツアー」のようになる

●音が弱くなる例―3

テル ゼム　　　　　　　　**テルエム**

<u>Tell them</u> I said hi.　→　<u>Tell 'em</u> I said hi.

* them はふつうは「ゼム」のように発音されるが、音が弱くなって先頭の [th] が落ちる
* カジュアルな発音では Tell'em とつながって「テルエム」のようになる。

●よく起きる「弱化」の例

tell him	→ tell 'im
ask her	→ ask 'er
let them	→ let 'em
what he	→ what 'e
something	→ somethin'
	→ some'm
can	→ c'n
for	→ f'r

from	→	fr'm
some	→	s'me

第2公式 音が短くなる「短縮」

英語では、音が短くなることがあります。語の音が弱く発音されて一部が消えてしまったり、特定の語と語がつながって発音の一部が省略されたりするからです。音が短くなることを**短縮**（たんしゅく）といいます。I've や That'd のように短縮された形を**短縮形**（たんしゅくけい）といいます。

●音が短くなる例—1

アイ ウイル　　アイル
I will get it. → I'll get it.

＊will の先頭が省略されて 'll と音が短くなる
＊音が省略された部分は '（アポストロフィー）で示される

●音が短くなる例—2

アイ ハヴ　　　　アイヴ
I have got to go. → I've got to go.

＊have の先頭が省略されて 've と音が短くなる
＊音が省略された部分は '（アポストロフィー）で示される

●音が短くなる例—3

　　アイ ウッド　　　　　　　　　アイド
　　<u>I would</u> be glad to.　→　I'd be glad to.

＊would の先頭が省略されて 'd と音が短くなる

＊音が省略された部分は '（アポストロフィー）で示される

●よく起きる「短縮」の例

＜主語 ＋ have動詞＞

I have	→	I've
you have	→	you've
they have	→	they've

＜主語 ＋ had＞

I had	→	I'd
you had	→	you'd
they had	→	they'd

＜主語 ＋ be動詞＞

I am	→	I'm
you are	→	you're
they are	→	they're

＜be動詞 ＋ not＞

are not	→	aren't
is not	→	isn't
was not	→	wasn't

＜主語 ＋ will＞

I will	→	I'll
you will	→	you'll
they will	→	they'll

＜主語 ＋ would＞

I would	→	I'd
you would	→	you'd
they would	→	they'd

＜助動詞 ＋ not＞

cannot	→	can't
will not	→	won't
could not	→	couldn't

＜疑問詞 ＋ be動詞/will＞

what are	→	what're
what is	→	what's
what will	→	what'll

第3公式　音がつながる「連結」

　英語では、語句の音と音がつながって発音されることがひんぱんにあります。特に子音と母音の組み合わせでは音がつながるのが自然で言いやすいからです。音がつながることを**連結**（れんけつ）または**リエゾン**といいます。

●音がつながる例—1

イン アン アワー

I'll be back in an hour.

イナナワー

→ I'll be back in an hour.

＊[n] [a] で「ナ」、[n] [a] で「ナ」

●音がつながる例—2

マインド イフ アイ　　**マインディファイ**

Mind if I join you?　→　Mind if I join you?

＊[d] [i] で「ディ」 [f] [ai] で「ファイ」

●音がつながる例—3

ギヴ イット ア　　**ギヴィラ**

I'll give it a try.　→　I'll give it a try.

＊[v] [i] で「ヴィ」 [t] [a] で「タ」から「ラ」

●よく起きる「連結」の例

[r] ＋母音

are all　　→　are all

figure it　→　figure it

[n] ＋母音

in order　→　in order

sign up　→　sign up

[d] ＋母音

should I　→　should I

find out　→　find out

[t] ＋母音

| set it | → | set_it |
| at all | → | at_all |

第4公式　音が消える「消失」

英語では、単語のなかの音が消えることが多々あります。英語のリズムの関係や [n] のあとに [t] が続くなど音の組み合わせで発音しやすいように消えてしまうのです。単語のなかの音が消えてしまうことを**消失**（しょうしつ）といいます。

●音が消える例—1

アバウト　　　　　　　**バウト**
How about you?　→　How 'bout you?

＊about は「バ」にアクセントがあるので、その前の「ア」は弱く発音される
＊「ア」がさらに弱くなって消えてしまうが、これがかなり一般的な発音

●音が消える例—2

プレンティ
We've got plenty of time.

プレニィ
→ We've got plen'y of time.

＊plenty には [n] [t] と続く音があり、[n] の影響で [t] が消えしまう

＊アメリカ英語では [n]+[t] の組み合わせで [t] が消えることが多い

●音が消える例—3

イグザクトリィ

That's <u>exactly</u> the point.

イグザク( )リィ

→ That's exac'ly the point.

＊exactly には [t] [l] と続く音があり、[l] の影響で [t] が消えしまう

＊[t] が消えても [t] を発音するために口を構える一瞬の間（ま）がある

●よく起きる「消失」の例

twenty	→	twe**n'**y
exactly	→	exa**c'**ly
certain	→	cer'**n**
doctor	→	do'tor
outside	→	ou'side
expect	→	'**x**pect
suppose	→	s'**p**pose
believe	→	**b'**lieve
suggest	→	s'**g**gest
different	→	diff**'r**ent
appreciate	→	'**p**preciate
friend	→	frien'

第5公式 音が抜け落ちる「脱落」

英語では、自然に話されるときに、単語と単語のつながりにおいて音が抜け落ちてなくなってしまうことが多々あります。同じ音や似た音を2度言うのは言いにくいので1つになったり、英語の強弱のリズムのせいで自然と音が抜け落ちるからです。

しかし、ただ抜け落ちるだけではなく、その場所に一瞬の間（ま）が取られます。語と語がつながるなかで音が抜け落ちることを**脱落**（だつらく）といいます。

● 音が抜け落ちる例—1

ハットティー　　　　　　**ハッ( )ティー**

I'll have hot tea.　→　I'll have ho' tea.

＊hot の [t] と day の [t] と同じ音が続いている
＊同じ音が続くと前の1つが抜け落ちる

● 音が抜け落ちる例—2

グッド ディ　　　　　　**グッ( )ディ**

Have a good day.　→　Have a goo' day.

＊good の [d] と day の [d] と同じ音が続いている
＊同じ音が続くと前の1つが抜け落ちる

● 音が抜け落ちる例—3

クッド ハヴ

I could have done that.

クダヴ
→ I could've done that.
　　クダ
→ I coulda done that.

＊could have は have の [h] が抜け落ちて could've（クダヴ）のようにつながる
＊さらに 've の [v] が抜け落ちて coulda（クダ）のようにつながる

●よく起きる「脱落」の例
<同じ音どうし>
　[m] [m]で前の音が脱落
　　some more　　→　so' more
　[l] [l] で前の [l] が脱落
　　I'll leave　　→　I' leave
　[t] [t] で前の [t] が脱落
　　hot tea　　→　ho' tea
　[k] [k] で前の [k] が脱落
　　take care　　→　ta' care

<似た音どうし>
　[g] [d] で [g] が脱落
　　big deal　　→　bi' deal
　　big diamond　→　bi' diamond
　[d] [t] で [d] が脱落
　　hard time　　→　har' time

[d] [p] で [d] が脱落

good place → goo' place

food processor → foo' processor

第6公式 音がとなりの音に似る「同化」

英語には、音がとなりの音に似ることがたくさんあります。ある音が、となりの音の影響を受けて、その音に似たり、同じ音になったりするケースがかなりあります。

2つの音がとなりあっているとき、一方が他方の影響を受けてとなりの音に似たり、同じ音になることを**同化**（どうか）といいます。

● 音がとなりの音に似る例—1

　　ハヴ トゥ　　　　　　　ハフタ
I <u>have to</u> go now. → I <u>hafta</u> go now.

＊have の [v] が to の [t] の影響を受けて、[f] に変わる
＊そして単語同士がつながって hafta（ハフタ）か hafto（ハフトゥ）のようになる

● 音がとなりの音に似る例—2

　　　　　　サポウズド トゥ
What's that <u>supposed to</u> mean?

　　　　　　サポウスタ
→ What's that <u>suppose'ta</u> mean?

＊supposed の [d] が to の [t] の影響を受けて、[t] に変わる

＊そして単語同士がつながって suppose'ta（サポウスタ）のようになる

●音がとなりの音に似る例―3

イン ゼア **インネア**

Put them in there. → Put them in 'ere.

＊in の [n] が there の [th] に影響を与えて [n] のように変える

＊すると [n] の音が2つ続くような感じになり in 'ere（インネア）のようになる

●よく起きる「同化」の例

<前の音が、後ろの音に影響を与えて同化>

[n] が [th] に影響を与え同じ [n] の音になる

in that → in 'at
down there → down 'ere
doin' that → doin 'at

<後ろの音が、前の音に影響を与えて同化>

[k] が [v] に影響を与えて [f] に変える

of course → off course

[t] が [v] に影響を与えて [f] に変える

have to → hafta/hafto

[t] が [d] に影響を与えて [t] に変える

used to → use'ta/use'to
pleased to → please'ta/please'to

[p] が [n] に影響を与えて [m] に変える

in person　　　→　im person
in public　　　→　im public

第7公式　音が別の音に変わる「融合同化」

英語では、自然に話されるときに、となりあった2つの音が互いに影響を与え合って第3の音を作り出すことが多々あります。となりあった2つの音を続けて発音すると口の構えから自然に別の音になるからです。

2つの隣り合った音が互いに影響しあって、別個の音（第3の音）に変化することを**融合同化**（ゆうごうどうか）といいます。

●音が別の音に変わる例—1

　　　　ミートユー　　　　　　　ミーチュ
Nice to meet you. → Nice to meetju.

＊[t] [j] の2つの音が互いに影響しあう
＊すると [tʃ] という新しい音（第3の音）に変化する

●音が別の音に変わる例—2

クッド ユー
Could you do me a favor?

クッジュ
→ Couldju do me a favor?

＊[d] [j] の2つの音が互いに影響しあう
＊すると [dʒ] という新しい音（第3の音）に変化する

●音が別の音に変わる例—3

　　　　ミス ユー　　　　　ミシュー

I'll miss you. → I'll misju.

＊[s] [j]の2つの音が互いに影響しあう

＊すると [ʃ] という新しい音（第3の音）に変化する

●よく起きる「融合同化」の例

makes you	→	makesju
hope you	→	hopju
make you	→	makju
as you	→	azju
give me	→	gimme
let me	→	lemme
going to	→	gonna
want to	→	wanna

■「ローマの休日」ではこう話されている

＊**第1公式**　音が弱くなる「弱化」

AOE: I've got them right here, somewhere.
　→ I've got 'em right here, somewhere.

＊**第2公式**　音が短くなる「短縮」

JOE: What is your hurry? There is lots of time.
　→ What's your hurry? There's lots of time.

＊第3公式　音がつながる「連結」

ANN:　May be <u>another hour</u>.

→　May be another'our.

＊第4公式　音が消える「消失」

JOE:　No, how <u>about</u> this?

→　No, how 'bout this?

＊第5公式　音が抜け落ちる「脱落」

IRV:　You must be <u>out of</u> your mind!

→　You must be outta your mind!

＊第6公式　音がとなりの音に似る「同化」

IRV:　I <u>got to</u> get up early.

→　I gotta get up early.

＊第7公式　音が別の音に変わる「融合同化」

HEN:　Oh, I think I know the <u>dress you</u> mean.

→　Oh, I think I know the dresju mean.

本書は、(株)プレーントラスト所有の映画フィルムより翻案化したものです。
本書は、2007年3月に小社より刊行した
『別冊宝島1398　名作映画で英会話シリーズ　ローマの休日』を
改訂・改題し、文庫化したものです。

宝島
SUGOI
文庫

名作映画を英語で読む ローマの休日（字幕対訳付）
（めいさくえいがをえいごでよむ ろーまのきゅうじつ（じまくたいやくつき））

2009年4月18日　第1刷発行

編著者	藤田英時
発行人	蓮見清一
発行所	株式会社 宝島社

〒102-8388　東京都千代田区一番町25番地
　　　　　電話：営業 03(3234)4621／編集 03(3239)5746
　　　　　http://tkj.jp
　　　　　振替：00170-1-170829　（株）宝島社
印刷・製本　中央精版印刷株式会社

乱丁・落丁本はお取り替えいたします
©Eiji Fujita 2009 Printed in Japan
First published 2007 by Takarajimasha, Inc.
ISBN 978-4-7966-7085-2